analog

SCIENCE FICTION

SPACE VIKING
A great new novel by H. Beam Piper

Through Eyes of Wonder

SCIENCE FICTION AND SCIENCE

BY BEN BOVA

▲ADDISON-WESLEY

Addisonian Press titles
by Ben Bova

Planets, Life & LGM
Man Changes the Weather
The Weather Changes Man
Through Eyes of Wonder

 An Addisonian Press Book

18603

Text Copyright©1975 by Ben Bova
Illustrations Copyright©1975 by Addison-Wesley Publishing Company
All Rights Reserved
Addison-Wesley Publishing Company, Inc.
Reading, Massachusetts 01867
Printed in the United States of America
First Printing

WZ/WZ   9/75   09206

Library of Congress Cataloging in Publication Data

Bova, Benjamin.
  Through eyes of wonder.

  "An Addisonian Press Book."
  SUMMARY: Discusses the relationship between science
and science fiction with examples from literature.
  1. Science fiction—History and criticism—Juvenile
literature. [1. Science fiction—History and criticism]
I. Title.
PN3448.S45B6   809.3'876   74-13893
ISBN 0-201-09206-9

Contents

To Barbara and Bob,
the best sister and brother
that anyone could ask for.

Thank You, Superman

CHAPTER ONE

Back when the world was so young that I was barely beginning to read, the first issue of *Action Comics* arrived at Archdeacon's Cigar Store, around the corner from my home in South Philadelphia. Ten cents was an amount of money that you asked for politely in those less-than-affluent days, but somehow I obtained the money and immediately spent it on a copy of the comic book.

The first story in it was the first installment of *Superman*. And the first garish drawing on the very first page changed my life completely.

It showed the planet Krypton exploding, while a small rocket carried the infant Superman toward Earth and safety.

In one drawing, I became hooked on astronomy, rocketry, and science fiction. For life.

Because that single drawing taught me an extremely important lesson. The world changes. Sometimes violently. Even the heavens that look so placid and eternal are in a constant process of change. And obviously, changes happen here on Earth all the time.

Science and science fiction. The two march side by side through my life. I learned about astronomy in the Fels Planetarium, where the dramatic presentations of the starry universe sent me scampering to libraries for more and deeper information. And in those libraries I also found John Carter, Warlord of Mars; Delos D. Harriman, the man who sold the Moon; and H. G. Wells' time traveller.

Science and science fiction. World War II began as I started second grade and ended with the explosion of an atomic bomb on Hiroshima when I was in junior high. Commercial television burst into our lives in the post-war period. I became a newspaper reporter and rejoiced when the Salk vaccine ended each summer's long casualty list of children killed and crippled by polio. And then came Project Vanguard and America's first attempts to place a man-made object in space.

Science and science fiction. The war had long been predicted in the stories I was reading. The atomic bomb was no surprise, nor was the Cold War that followed; dozens of SF stories had dealt with both possibilities all through the 1930's and 40's. The conquest of disease was also standard fare in science fiction, and television had been predicted half a century earlier—although television commercials went beyond the worst nightmares of any SF writer.

I left the newspaper game and became a technical editor on Project Vanguard. I watched helplessly while Sputnik became humankind's first artificial satellite, and an overpressured Vanguard crew tried to respond to the hysterics of political leaders who had badly underestimated the importance of space exploration and consistently belittled research efforts. The first Vanguard attempt at a satellite launching ended four meters off the pad when the faulty first-stage rocket engine exploded. But four months later, on St. Patrick's Day, 1958, the Vanguard crew put a small satellite in orbit, and all of us connected with the project went into orbit right along with it.

The world around me was the world I had been reading about in science fiction. Then I stopped and realized that everyone else was living in the same world, too. The real world and the science fiction world had become one and the same for all of us. Science and technology had become prime movers in everyone's life.

I had been writing stories quite unsuccessfully for many years. But finally a novel of mine was published, and then I began to sell stories with some regularity. Meanwhile I was working daytimes with the Massachusetts Institute of Technology physics department and later at Avco Everett Research Laboratory. My "regular" working day involved me in explanations of interstellar distance measurements, gas and plasma physics, lasers, superconducting magnets, magnetohydrodynamics, and artificial hearts. It was sometimes hard to tell where the science ended and the fiction began.

But much more fascinating than the concepts and contraptions, were the people whom I came in contact with. I worked with marvelously interesting scientists and engineers, and quickly learned that they aren't much like those portrayed in many stories and most films. And I soon realized that science fiction was the best medium for showing to the general reading public just how scientists work and live.

Fifteen years have passed since those tense, exciting days of the Vanguard Project. Today the daily headlines clamor about an energy crisis, war in the Middle East, electronic "bugging," and space missions of longer duration and complexity than any of us would have dared hope for fifteen years ago. Men have walked on the Moon's surface, deliberately altered the weather here on Earth, searched for our origins as a species and for the possibilities of life elsewhere in the universe.

And the world that we read about and wrote about in science fiction continues to unfold in reality. The famines stemming from overpopulation are beginning in Asia and Africa. Our supplies of fossil fuels are running out, supplies that took 200 million years to produce and less than three centuries to deplete. Serious scientists have examined the way our civilization is behaving, and they predict total disaster for the whole human race unless we drastically alter our society, and alter it very soon.

The term "future shock" has been coined to show that most people are stunned by the enormity and rapidity of the changes boiling over us. And most of these changes have their roots in new developments of science and technology. The science fiction people have seen these changes coming for many years, and although they have been so far powerless to avert them, at least they seem to understand them. They are not quite as afraid of tomorrow as other people, because the most frightening thing about the future is that it is unknown. Science fiction readers have seen many futures, and whichever one actually comes to pass, it won't be a complete stranger to the science fiction audience.

This book will try to show how science and science fiction are related. Hopefully, we will see how

the beauties and wonder of science are translated into the exciting stories of science fiction, and how the power and danger of modern technology are critically examined in science fiction stories.

Many writers have made the point that the *only* people who will be able to deal successfully with the future are those who are prepared to accept change, and work for the kinds of changes that are desirable. Science fiction is one way to set your mind on the future, and prepare yourself for the changes that tomorrow will bring.

But to see why this is true, we must first look far back into the past.

The Urge to Know

CHAPTER TWO

The American astronomer Harlow Shapley (1885–1972) once said, "The urge to know has evolved from an instinct to a profession."

The urge to know. Curiosity.

Is curiosity an instinct that humans have? Certainly it is now a profession, as Shapley said. Science is, at heart, organized curiosity—a carefully developed way of finding out knowledge about the world around us and inside us.

If curiosity is an instinct, then the question is: Why do we have such an instinct? What good is it? And when did we acquire it?

The evidence on hand leads to the conclusion that curiosity existed in our remote ancestors long before they became fully human. And they developed it not merely as an idle plaything to fill in their quiet afternoons. For our remote ancestors, curiosity meant the difference between life and death. If they hadn't been curious, we wouldn't be here.

We wouldn't recognize our earliest direct ancestors as any relatives of ours. In fact, there are still many people who flatly refuse to believe that we humans are "descended from the apes." But the evidence shows very clearly that the human race developed from other forms of animals. Not apes. It's actually much less noble than that. Our most remote, direct ancestors looked more like mice than men.

(Notice we are saying *direct* ancestors here. All life on Earth is related, so in a way all earlier forms of life were ancestors of ours. But here we will speak only of those mammals that led eventually to the type of creature we ourselves are: *Homo sapiens sapiens*, Thinking Man.)

Our earliest, direct ancestors were tree shrews, and they looked pretty much like mice. In fact, some scientists believe that the rodents of those far-gone days, some 50 to 70 million years ago, fared much better than did our ancestors, who are called *prosimians* (meaning, "before the apes"). The rodents dominated the fields, the grasslands, and other ground terrain. The prosimians couldn't compete with them on the ground, so they took to the trees. There were rodents there, too, such as squirrels. But in general the tree shrews and other prosimian species were able to survive in the leafy world above the rodent-dominated ground.

Now wait a minute, you say. How can scientists claim they know what was happening 70 million years ago?

Aha! Your curiosity is aroused. Good.

We won't go into all the details of the way scientists weigh evidence in this chapter. But *paleontologists*, the men and women who study extinct forms of life, have been digging up fossil remains of long-dead creatures for more than a century now.

The fossilized bones of the prosimians show that their bodies were adapted for living in trees. Their paws were made for gripping branches, not for running on the relatively flat ground. The claws that rodents have for digging have changed into gripping fingers in the prosimians. The eyes have moved to the front of the head where they can provide overlapping, stereo vision—which is absolutely essential when your life depends on accurately judging the distance between the branch you're on and the one you're going to jump to. A mistake and you tumble down to the ground, to injury or death. Prosimians that didn't have good depth perception (which depends on stereo vision) didn't live long.

Curiosity was an important trait for those earliest ancestors of ours. Living up in the branches of tall trees, they couldn't see very far around them because of the leaves that surrounded them. And there were always life-or-death questions facing them, such as: Is this branch strong enough to hold me if I go out to the end and try to get that luscious-looking piece of fruit hanging there?

The prosimians—and their monkey and ape descendents—learned to coordinate their forepaws and eyes very closely. Which is something we still do today. We look before we touch. And when we see something interesting, we reach out for it so that we can bring it close to us for a thorough examination. NASA engineers speak of "eyeballing the problem." The prosimians did the same.

Among their problems was the ever present danger of falling. And there was a predator that also lived in the trees: the snake. Today, humans have an instinctive fear of falling, and most people react automatically with fear or dislike to snakes.

Curiosity was a good and healthy instinct for these tree dwellers. They had to be constantly on the lookout for food and danger. And the leafy world of the tall trees, windswept and always changing, must have been quite a bit different from life on the ground. On the ground, everything was more stable and predictable.

Ground dwelling creatures didn't develop curiosity, or at least not to the degree that the tree dwellers did. They dug holes for themselves, instead.

Somewhere around 25 million years ago, our ancestors left the trees and began to live on the ground. No one can say for certain why this happened, but there are at least two important contributing factors.

First, our ancestors had grown large. From the mouse-like size of the tree shrews, they had become more like modern monkeys and chimpanzees in size. Their fossilized bones, skulls, and teeth show that they were getting too big to go scampering around in the high branches of the forest world.

And the forests were getting smaller. Climate conditions were changing. The whole Earth itself was in upheaval then, throwing up mountain chains such as the Rockies and Himalayas. The worldwide forests of the earlier era dwindled. There wasn't enough room among the trees for all the types of creatures that had once lived in their shelter.

So our ancestors took to the grasslands. They can now be called *hominids*, man-like creatures. But we would scarcely think so, to look at them. They resembled rather large monkeys rather than human beings.

But living on the ground forced them to change. They learned to walk erect, and the fossil evidence shows that their feet and legs changed and became human-looking long before the rest of their bodies, faces, or brains did.

They had some important advantages over other ground dwelling creatures, thanks to their earlier ages in the trees. The hominids had hands that could grasp, and eyes that could see better than any creature on the ground.

Soon they became hunters. They learned how to use animal bones for tools: primitive clubs, scrapers for taking the hide off the animal they were going to eat, even needles of a sort for sewing those hides into warm garments.

Curiosity must have been an invaluable help in this strange time of learning to live on the ground. Curiosity and its close cousin, alertness. Many species were forced to leave the dwindling forests, and died in the attempt. The hominids, our ancestors, made the change. They themselves were enormously changed, physically. Even their brains began to change and grow.

And then, about a half million years ago, curiosity made its greatest discovery: fire.

The hominids had evolved by that time into a creature that we now call *Homo erectus*, erect-standing man. He was only about five feet tall at his most erect, and his brain was only about two-thirds the size of our own.

But he was curious.

If you've ever stared into a campfire, or the crackling logs in a fireplace, you know how fascinating the flickering, ever changing flames can be. *Homo erectus* must have been equally fascinated. When a volcano's molten lava set grass and trees on fire, or a terrifying bolt of lightning turned a bush into a torch, some member of the *erectus* species must have overcome his very understandable fear long enough to reach out for the bright, hypnotic flames.

No telling how many times our ancestors were rewarded with nothing more than a sharp pain and a yelp of fear. But eventually someone, somewhere, learned how to handle fire safely.

And the entire history of planet Earth was changed at that precise moment.

Before fire, our ancestors were merely another form of animal trying to survive in the changing climates of those early times. An Ice Age gripped the world and covered vast areas with frozen glaciers. But with fire, the hominids and their descendents—we humans—not only survived, but dominated the world. We spread to every part of the world, except for Antarctica, which had been separated by vast ocean stretches from all the other land masses of Earth many ages before.

Thanks to fire. Thanks to curiosity.

And thanks also to a way of living that made wandering a necessity. For as our ancestors learned to become hunters, they learned to follow the herds of game animals on their migrations. They had no fixed place of abode, no single spot that they called home. Where the meat animals went, our hunting ancestors went also.

During the Ice Age the world's climate seemed to go haywire. Huge glaciers ground down from the pole and from mountaintops to cover much of the land with layers of ice more than two kilometers thick. Patterns of rain and dry seasons that had lasted for eons were totally disrupted. Many species of plant and animal life died off, unable to stand the wild changes in climate. Four times the glaciers covered the world with winters that lasted 10,000 years and more. Four times they retreated and there reigned a worldwide summer, with temperatures much warmer than our present global climate.

The game herds migrated over vast distances, searching for the kinds of climate in which they could survive. Man, the hunter, followed them.

Thus man became not merely a nomadic hunter, but a world traveller. Dressed in animal skins and carrying the knowledge of fire, our ancestors—who were by this time *Homo sapiens sapiens*, as are we—walked across Africa, Europe and Asia. They crossed land bridges into America and Australia. They covered the Earth.

Think for a moment about the grandest adventure tales you can recall. How many of them involved fantastic journeys across unknown lands and seas? Think of the greatest heroes of history and myth: Jason and the Argonauts, Sinbad the Sailor, Leif Erikson, Marco Polo, Prince Henry the Navigator, Columbus, Lewis and Clarke, Peary, Lindbergh, the Apollo astronauts, the people who will reach Mars. . .

Curiosity, the urge to see new lands, to set foot where no man has stepped before, has given the human race some of its greatest stories.

And this same curiosity, this exact urge to see new worlds, to learn new things, is the basic drive behind science and scientific research. To understand what makes the sun shine, how to cure cancer, what lies inside the smallest elementary particle, what our beginning might have been—all these questions of science stem from the curiosity that's been with us since long before we were entirely human.

But of all the questions that have puzzled and troubled humans and pre-humans, the most perplexing must have been the question of death.

Anthropologists—the scientists who study humankind itself—have unearthed grave sites that date well back into the Ice Age. Not only did our immediate ancestors bury their dead, but so did another type of human, the Neanderthals.

Homo sapiens neanderthalis existed for about 100,000 to 200,000 years. The Neanderthals arose before the Ice Age, but by the end of the last glaciation—a scant 10,000 years ago—there were no more of them left. The only type of human remaining on Earth was our own *Homo sapiens sapiens*.

The Neanderthals looked a bit different from ourselves. Their skulls were flatter and longer and broader. They had thick bony ridges over their eye sockets, and hardly any chin at all. Their arms and legs tended to be shorter but heavier, and probably stronger, than our own. Their brains were as large as ours, though. And when the cold millennia of the Ice Age were at their peak, the Neanderthals had developed tools and used fire just as our immediate ancestors did.

And they buried their dead. Buried them surrounded by their tools and hunting weapons, often decorated with flowers. In other words, they apparently believed in some form of life after death, where the dead person would need his favorite implements.

There was no way for even the most curious human to explore the world of life-after-death. As Shakespeare's Hamlet says, that is "the unknown country, from whose bourne no traveller returns."

But primitive humans must have seen the connection between illness, injury, and death. The early medicine men, whom anthropologists usually call *shaman* from a Sanskrit word, dealt both with healing the sick or injured and with the spirit world of life-beyond-death. The shaman thus started two professions simultaneously: scientist and priest. As we'll see, it wasn't until the Copernican Revolution, a scant 500 years ago, that science and religion became separated.

By the end of the last glaciation, some 10,000 years ago, human beings had invented agriculture. They learned that they could deliberately plant the seeds of certain grains and harvest a crop after it grew to maturity.

This was world-shaking.

For the first time, our ancestors could stop roaming after the game herds and could literally make food grow up out of the ground. It was miraculous to them. And it seemed quite clear that there was a strong connection between planting, growing, and harvesting their crops and the birth, life, and death of a person.

The connection between the life cycle of the crops and the life cycle of a human being was obvious to these early farmers. Also, the need to predict the proper time for planting and harvesting was critically important. For the first time in human history, people's food supply became directly dependent on the weather. Not just the climate, which might bring an occasional drought that forced the game herds, and their human hunters, to migrate to an area that was better watered. Farming made human beings dependent on the day-to-day weather.

A rainstorm at the wrong time could rot the seed in the ground, before it got a chance to sprout. A hot dry spell in the middle of the growing season could stunt the crop or wither it, leaving little grain for the coming winter. A storm just before harvest could destroy the fruits of an entire growing season's labor.

The shaman of the hunting society became the astronomer-priests of the agricultural societies. The animal totems of the hunters gave way to the gods and goddesses of the weather and the fields: sun, rain, fertility.

The connection between human life and a good harvest became a part of the religious beliefs. If there was bad weather and the crops fared poorly, obviously it was because someone in the group had angered the gods. After all, it was human activity that planted and harvested the crops, wasn't it? Then it must be human activity of some sort that blighted them. In some areas of the world, including the land we now call Greece, the local community's ruler was ritually murdered each spring and his blood sprinkled on the fields to ensure a good crop. For just as the old grain had to die before the new grain could grow, the human sacrifice had to offer up his life for the good of the community. This became a key part of many religions.

The priests of those times did more than practice bloody rituals. They were astronomer-priests. They learned how to watch the heavens and predict the seasons of the year. They found that the stars are very precise timekeepers as they march around the sky, rank on rank, night after night. They never change, and year after year they will announce the coming of planting time, and harvest time, if a man is wise enough to read the signs.

(Actually, the stars do change, but over such enormously long periods of time that it never mattered to the astronomer-priests of 10,000 years ago.)

The power to predict the seasons was an awesome power indeed, back in those *Neolithic* times when farming was new and humans were first beginning to build the fixed settlements that would eventually become villages and cities. Why else would hard working farmers allow some of their fellow-men to do absolutely no work at all, except for star gazing and performing religious rituals? Back in the days when all men were hunters, even the shaman had to get his own food. Primitive hunting societies that still exist today work that way. But in the early agricultural societies, the astronomer-priests did not go out to plow the fields. Their "field" was in the sky.

Agriculture was a great success, and before too many millennia passed, humans had built cities and kingdoms and even empires. The glories of ancient Greece and the grandeur of the Roman Empire were based on the ability to grow the wheat that fed millions of citizens (a word that literally means *city dweller*).

Organized agriculture allowed humans to feed many more people from the same area of land than hunting could ever allow. For example, the American Indians of North America probably never totalled more than a million people, spread in hunting tribes over the entire continent. Yet in Mexico and Peru, where agriculture was organized, millions lived in a few cities.

With plenty of food from farming and a booming population, you'd think that human curiosity had paid off handsomely. And it had. But that didn't satisfy the urge to know. There were always more questions than answers.

For example: The heavens were a miracle of order and perfection. The stars marched around in perfect order, never moving out of place, never changing their brightness. Except that once in a while a star seemed to fall out of the heavens; a brilliant meteor would streak across the sky, startling all who saw it.

And then on rare occasions a comet would show up, and hang in the sky like a pointing finger. Pointing to what? Something dreadful that's going to happen, obviously!

Worst of all, there were five stars that flatly refused to stay put in the heavens. They wandered around restlessly, and in fact were ultimately named "wanderers," *planetos*, by the ancient Greeks.

Stars that can defy all the logic and order of the heavens must obviously be the most powerful entities in the sky. So each society named the planets after their gods and goddesses. We know them by their Roman names: Mercury, Venus, Mars, Jupiter and Saturn.

How can it be that these stars move around while all the others stay fixed in their ordained places? Curious humans constructed elaborate theories to explain that. And to check on their theories, they tried to determine if the theories could predict what the planets would do next.

Prediction: That is the essence of all knowledge. If a piece of information can be used to make a successful prediction, then it is knowledge. If it can't predict, then it's gossip, or unproven theory, or a waste of time.

Ancient Greek astronomers constructed a system for the heavens that predicted where the planets would be at any given time, and it worked fairly well. It was a complex system, and it assumed that the Earth is at the center of the universe, and all the stars revolve around us. This is a perfectly natural assumption. Even though we know that it's wrong.

However, the predictions that you can make using the so-called *Ptolemaic* system are pretty good. So the system lasted for some long time: nearly two thousand years. Since it was based on the idea that the Earth is at the center of the universe, it's also called a *geocentric* system. (Geo, for Earth.)

But the Ptolemaic system was complicated. And as astronomers learned how to make more and more accurate observations of the planets' positions in the sky, it was seen that the Ptolemaic system's predictions were farther and farther out of line with the actual observed positions of the planets. To bring the system into better agreement with the observations, the system was made even more complicated.

Then from Poland came a timid suggestion for a solution to the problem. Nicholas Copernicus (1473–1543) was curious about the heavens. Although he was a civil employee of the Catholic Church, his main interest in life was explaining why those five planets behaved the way they did. He hit upon a simple and elegant answer: The universe is not geocentric but *heliocentric.* The planets— including Earth—revolve around the sun.

To us today this seems an obvious truth. Yet you'd be quite hard put to prove it without looking for the answers in a physics or astronomy text.

In the Sixteenth Century, the Copernican concept was literally breathtaking. It was revolutionary. Copernicus himself knew that the Church and most of the authoritative thinkers of that day would reject his idea. He only agreed to have his work published as a book when he was on his death bed.

For no matter how modestly Copernicus stated his idea, (and he wrote that it was merely an interesting speculation), it *was* truly revolutionary. It said that the Earth is not the center of all creation. It flew in the face of the teachings of the Church, which had backed the Ptolemaic geocentric system for centuries, as a matter of course. The Church was unwilling to admit that it might be wrong, and the battle line between religion and science was drawn up, and the arguments raged.

It was a fierce battle, although a needless one. Both sides were earnestly trying to seek the truth, but both sides accused the "enemy" of being blindly stubborn. Men actually died in this battle, burned at the stake as heretics.

The Copernican idea eventually won, even though there were many things wrong with it. The "bugs" were worked out, over the years, by other astronomers and scientists and philosophers.

The knockout blow against the Ptolemaic system was delivered by the Italian scientist Galileo Galilei (1564–1642) in the year 1609. That summer he heard about the invention of the telescope, and quickly built a crude instrument for himself. Legend has it he sawed a piece of pipe from a church organ to form the tube for the instrument. Instead of looking at distant mountains or steeples, however, Galileo pointed his telescope at the sky. That's the difference between talent and genius. What he saw there destroyed the geocentric theory forever.

You can see it too, with a decent pair of binoculars: the four major moons of Jupiter. To this day they're called Jupiter's *Galilean satellites*.

Here were four moons circling another planet, Jupiter. They were not going around Earth at all. If they aren't centered on the Earth, it proves that not everything in the universe revolves around Earth.

Galileo also saw that the planets are different from the stars. They show disks, while the true stars remain merely pinpoints of light. And Venus goes through phases like the Moon, just as Copernicus had predicted. And the Moon is far from being a smooth, perfect sphere as the Ptolemaic theories had insisted it must be: It showed rough mountains and craters. Even the sun shows spots on its face, whereas Ptolemaic thinkers had decided that all heavenly bodies must be perfect and pure.

Galileo ran into trouble with the Church authorities over his vigorous and cantankerous championing of these new and frightening (to them) ideas. He was forced to say publically that he was wrong. Yet the reality of his observations were there for anyone to see.

Meanwhile, in England another many-talented and troubled man was laying the groundwork for an organized way of conducting scientific research, a technique that has since come to be known as *the scientific method*. The man was Francis Bacon (1561–1626), and his idea is called *inductive reasoning*. That is a method of thought in which a large number of bits and pieces of evidence, clues, are put together to form a new piece of knowledge.

For example, thanks to Galileo and others, scientists learned that all bodies fall at the same rate of speed, no matter what their weight. Legend has it that Galileo proved this to his own satisfaction by hauling two iron balls up to the top of the Leaning Tower of Pisa. One of the balls was much larger and heavier than the other. He dropped them simultaneously, they fell at exactly the same speed, and they hit the ground together.

The reason that a feather doesn't fall at the same speed as a hammer, Galileo concluded, is that the feather literally floats on air; it's light enough for the air to impede its fall. In a vacuum they would both fall at the same speed. Three centuries later, our Apollo astronauts proved this by dropping a feather and a hammer on the airless surface of the Moon, in a demonstration televised back to Earth. The feather and the hammer hit the lunar soil at the same instant.

Galileo, incidentally, hit on one of the most vital ideas of modern science: measurement. Instead of arguing about how bodies fall, as philosophers had for centuries, he climbed Pisa's tower and *measured* the phenomenon. One of the major differences between science and meaningless chatter is that scientific work insists on measurement.

To get back to our example of inductive reasoning: Galileo showed an important truth about falling bodies. Meanwhile, Johannes Kepler (1571–1630) was working out the laws governing the motions of the planets as they go around the sun. Using the extremely detailed observations by the Danish astronomer Tycho Brahe (1564–1601), Kepler showed that the planets moved around the sun in elliptical orbits, rather than circular ones. Up until this time, it had been automatically assumed that everything in the heavens moved in perfect circles.

In England, Isaac Newton (1642–1727) took the work of Galileo and Kepler and produced a monumental idea: the concept of universal gravitation. Gravity. Every object in the whole universe attracts every other object. The Earth attracts a falling apple, the sun attracts the Earth and holds it in its yearly orbit, and stars attract each other.

By using inductive reasoning, going from one clue to another and building a constantly-enlarging scheme of ideas, three generations of scientists were able to go from a pair of iron balls dropped off a lopsided tower to the discovery of the force that binds the entire universe together.

That is the scientific method: inductive reasoning, using theories that give voice to new ideas, and experiments that test the validity of the theories. Organized curiosity utilizes measurement instead of rhetoric, logic instead of authority.

Today we take all this pretty much for granted. But every time a scientist comes up with a startling new notion, he's got to fight the same old forces of doubt and fear all over again. When Charles Darwin (1809–1882) hit on the idea of evolution—the concept that plant and animal species change from one form to another, just as we have evolved from a long line of prosimian and hominid ancestors—he was vilified by the public and ridiculed by other scientists who refused to accept his views. Yet, over the years, the overwhelming weight of evidence made even his strongest opponents among the scientists grudgingly admit that evolution is a valid idea. The scientists accepted the evidence that they saw; yet today, many non-scientists still cannot accept the idea of evolution, for emotional or religious reasons.

Much the same thing happened to Sigmund Freud (1856–1939) who pioneered the psychiatric study of the mind.

Scientists are not coldly logical thinking machines who speak only in jargon and equations. They argue, often fiercely. But they argue about evidence that can be measured. They argue about interpretation of measurements. And this is fine. Because it is only by argument—*rational* argument, the clash of opposing views and the presentation of evidence to support those views—that people can learn. No one learns anything when everyone agrees.

But while scientists have been scratching at humanity's itch to know and explore, many human beings have feared and even hated science and the men who practice it. Since those Ice Age days of tribal shamans, many people have held mixed feelings about the medicine man, the astronomer-priest, the wizard, the scientist.

On the one hand, most people envied his special knowledge and skills. They sought to use his power for their own gain. "Heal my child . . . hurt my enemy . . . bring prosperity to my crops . . . build me a better cannon . . . design a more destructive bomb . . . find a cure for this disease . . . invent a product that will make me rich." These are the kinds of things that the shaman-turned-scientist has been asked to do, over the ages.

On the other hand, these same people who used the scientist feared his power, hated the fact that he knew more than they did, and often believed he was in league with supernatural forces of evil.

Even today, people tend to hold scientists in awe. Scientists are given credit for bringing us nuclear power, modern medicines, space flight, and under-arm deodorants. They are blamed for pollution, overpopulation, war, and many other social ills that are not their fault at all. Yet at the same time we see scientists laughed at, and shown in movies or on television either as fuzzy-brained eggheads or coldly ruthless makers of monsters.

Scientists are a minority group in today's society, and like most minority groups they're largely hidden from the public's sight. They're tucked away in ghettos—laboratories, university campuses, field sites. They are quietly pursuing the eons-old urge to know. What makes a star collapse? How does the human brain work? Can we predict earthquakes? Can we control the weather?

Scientists are people, and they are pursuing the most human activity we can imagine. They are neither eggheads nor monster makers, although there is the same ratio of fools and schemers among them as there is among any group of human beings.

Scientists have the same emotions, needs, hopes, and fears that all humans have. But before the great majority of people can understand this, they must learn something about science and scientists. They must get to know the beauties and wonders of scientific thought. They must get to know the essential humanity of the men and women who devote their lives to scientific research.

One excellent way that large numbers of people—particularly young people—are finding out about science and scientists is by reading stories that deal with these subjects. Not dry textbooks, or biographies, or history books. Fiction. Made-up adventures and dramas that show the universe of science and the people who live in that universe:

Science fiction.

"What if....?"

CHAPTER THREE

For generations, librarians and teachers have felt uncomfortable about science fiction.

After all, they reasoned, it is obviously pulp literature. And therefore trash. Lurid magazine covers with half-naked blonde girls being attacked by giant lobsters. Stupid movies in which half-naked redheads are attacked by giant grasshoppers. Once in a *very* great while, a literary critic would condescend to review a science fiction book, holding his nose and gritting his teeth all the while.

There was a sort of motto: "If it's science fiction, it can't be good. If it's good, it can't be science fiction."

There *were* some science fiction writers who produced books of unquestioned excellence. H. G.

Wells and Jules Verne, for example. But they were regarded as Founding Fathers; nobody writing in modern days could produce anything good that was science fiction. Well, there was Aldous Huxley's *Brave New World* and George Orwell's *1984*, but those books weren't really science fiction. They couldn't be. They were *good.*

Yet the kids loved science fiction, kept buying those magazines with the lurid covers, and kept pestering their librarians for more science fiction books. Science fiction has been especially popular among teen-aged and pre-teen boys. Thankfully, in today's more liberated social environment, it's becoming equally popular among the girls.

Before we go any further, we ought to be sure that we understand just what we mean by the term, "science fiction."

There's no surer way to get two science fiction fans fighting than to ask them to define just what science fiction is. As Nikita Krushchev once said about physicists: "You ask ten physicists a question, and you get twelve different answers."

Science fiction is a tremendously broad field of literature. In fact, many people today prefer to use the term, "SF," which can be taken to mean "science fiction," or "science fantasy," or "speculative fiction," or even (hold on now!) "scientific fantabulation."

Some people would say that science fiction includes outright fantasies about the supernatural and enchanted princesses. There's an entire branch of SF called "sword and sorcery." These stories are usually set in a far-ancient time, and draw some of their inspiration from legends such as those of King Arthur. J. R. R. Tolkien's immensely popular Ring Trilogy and Hobbits books are put into the SF category by the publishing industry. But to the publishers, SF is a term of convenience for merchandizing. If it's not a book about the here-and-now or historical fiction, they'll throw it into the SF bin.

On the other end of the scale, there are those who would scorn the "SF" title and use only the term, "science fiction." With the accent on the *science*. To them, science fiction stories deal only with themes that involve futuristic science or technology: robots, star ships, lasers, computers. They look for functioning hardware and interesting gimmicks. Most SF people call this end of the field, "hard core science fiction."

Then there's a whole area in the middle that contains stories dealing with mental telepathy and other aspects of ESP, stories about the politics of future societies, stories that are short on the physical sciences such as physics and astronomy and deal instead with social sciences such as anthropology and sociology.

All these story types, throughout the broad spectrum of SF, have certain things in common.

They are not about the here-and-now world.

They deal with ideas. New ideas.

They show that the world of the future (or distant past) will be (or was) very different from today.

In other words, SF stories deal with *change*. From the wildest "sword and sorcery" fantasy to the sternest stainless steel "hard core" story, science fiction is a literature of ideas, and THE literature of change.

More than any other type of fiction published in this century, science fiction has addressed itself to that very human urge to know.

Stories that deal with the vastness of the starry universe, stories that speculate about intelligent beings on other worlds, stories that show how men and women might react to anything and everything from nuclear war to a drug that gives them immortality. Science fiction allows its readers to explore the entire universe of space and time, to answer that ageless question, "What would happen if . . .?"

In this chapter, and throughout this book, when we speak of science fiction, we'll be talking about those stories in which some aspect of science or technology plays a vital role. This eliminates the more fantasy-oriented side of the broad SF field, but it includes a wider scope than the strictest interpretation of the "hard core" enthusiasts would allow.

Year after year, young readers have demanded science fiction from their librarians. For decades they have bought science fiction magazines with a zeal that approaches religious faith. And when paperback books first became available, they made science fiction one of the strongest *genres* in the paperback publishing business.

An astute teacher or librarian might have wondered what there was in science fiction that attracted young readers. But as recently as a few years ago, I had a librarian tell me, "I don't know what they see in it! I never read any of it myself, of course, but the youngsters are *fascinated* by it."

Never read any of it. *Never!*

Some teachers were even worse, until rather recently. Teachers of English tended to gag over the words, "science fiction." They felt that *Silas Marner* and *The Mill on the Floss* were "good" books, despite the fact that no one has read such books outside of an English class assignment since approximately 1919. Yet they tended to regard science fiction as "pulp literature," or "pop literature." They might put up with it, but they certainly didn't recommend it for serious reading.

Teachers of science were equally turned off to science fiction, because they regarded most of what passed for science in the stories as outrageous gobbledygook. Teachers of social studies, history and other subjects simply maintained an intense disinterest in science fiction.

Today the situation is very much reversed.

Science fiction stories are being used in social studies classes as a means of teaching social values and showing how societies change.

At conventions of English teachers, whole seminars have been devoted to science fiction topics.

Several hundred colleges and universities are offering courses in science fiction. These courses are usually overfilled and students must be turned away. Science fiction writers are invited to lecture at auditoria jammed with students from all walks of campus life: English majors, historians, ROTC officers, and student radical activists. No one has yet been able to figure out how many high schools and junior highs are now giving short courses in science fiction—usually at the demands of the students.

An organization of teachers and researchers has been formed specifically for SF, and is called the Science Fiction Research Association.

And in my office at *Analog* magazine, hardly a week goes by when I'm not asked to assist a teacher who's putting together a science fiction course, or a student who's researching a term paper on the subject.

Why is science fiction so popular now? Well, it always has been popular among a fair share of the students. Why is it just now becoming recognized by their teachers and librarians? Why wasn't it accepted as an important part of modern literature years earlier? There are many theories.

Certainly the success of the Apollo program showed many people that "shooting for the Moon" was no longer an impossible dream. And our growing realization that many of our most pressing problems—pollution, population, peace—all depend very strongly on science and technology has also helped to turn the spotlight on science fiction.

But an important part of the answer to science fiction's newfound respectability is very simple: The young readers are finally getting what they've wanted all along. Our society has finally moved into the position where young peoples' voices are being listened to. And the young people want science fiction.

Why? Also an easily-answered question. One of the favorite aphorisms of today's generations is, "Tomorrow is the first day of the rest of your life." Science fiction is the literature of tomorrow. It deals with the future. It speaks of the changes that will come to our society, to other societies, to the human race as a whole, to the individual human being him or herself. Science fiction paints on a gigantic canvas that includes all of the universe of space and stars, all of time from beginning to end, and the whole universe inside the mind of *Homo sapiens sapiens*. There are no foreign lands in science fiction. There are no forbidden subjects. The fears and hopes of today's youth are laid bare and examined. The path of the future is charted.

How can it be that the kids were right all along about science fiction, and their elders were wrong? What actually happened was that the elders—from librarians to book publishers—were the victims of a cultural gap.

To understand how this situation came about, we must delve briefly into the history of science fiction.

Historians of literature have pointed out that many of the great figures of letters have tried their hands at what might loosely be called science fiction, from time to time. Indeed, Cyrano de Bergerac began the modern era of science fiction in his tales of journeys to the sun and Moon. Some of his tongue-in-cheek ideas were used by Edmund Rostand in his play about Cyrano.

L. Sprague de Camp, a science fiction writer and historian, has pointed out that just about *all* of literature dealt with fantasy and other-worldly romance until Cervantes wrote *Don Quixote* (in 1605), which was the first book to cast a realistic eye at the world in which people really lived.

Most of the writers that students are assigned to read—Dickens, de Foe, Stevenson, Poe, and others—wrote stories of wild fantasy or outright science fiction at one time or another. By the latter decades of the Nineteenth Century English literature was rife with so-called *scientific romances,* popular stories in which scientific discoveries or technological inventions were key features of the background and plot.

Out of this scene stepped Jules Verne and H. G. Wells, who until rather recently were the only "respectable" writers of science fiction known to most adults.

But on the American side of the Atlantic, other forces were at work shaping a ghetto for science fiction.

By the beginning of the Twentieth Century, pulp magazines were an important part of the American publishing industry. They used the cheapest paper and printing available, and sold for the lowest popular prices. People called them "penny dreadfuls" and "dime novels." They filled the role, in those years, that television fills today. They were packed with hastily-written stories that emphasized romance and adventure, and were always treating their readers to scenes in darkest Africa, the wild West, on the high seas, or remotest Asia.

One enterprising man, Hugo Gernsback, started to include science fiction stories in the pulp magazines he ran. In 1926 he brought out a new magazine totally devoted to science fiction. He called it *Amazing Stories*. Although it has gone through many changes in ownership, format and editors, *Amazing* is still being published today, the oldest science fiction magazine in the world.

Amazing was enough of a success to convince rival publishers that they should enter this "new" field of science fiction. Soon newsstands were flooded with *Wonder Stories, Astounding Stories of Super-Science, Startling* magazines—and more. For the most part they were out-and-out copies of *Amazing*.

And they were terrible!

By modern standards, most of the stories in these science fiction pulps were unbelievably poor. Some were stiff lectures by a character who was labelled a brilliant scientist. His assistant and beautiful daughter would hold hands while Dr. Scientist talked endlessly about his latest invention. The so-called "science" was almost always nearly-pure nonsense.

At the other end of the scale were the adventure stories that could have been written for any kind of pulp magazine. Indeed, many pulp writers sold virtually identical stories time and again to science fiction, western, detective, and other types of magazines. All they did was to change the cowboy's Stetson to a space helmet, change the six gun to a ray gun, the western plains to the deserts of Mars, and the Apaches to the six-legged Martians.

July, 1926

25 Cents

AMAZING STORIES

HUGO GERNSBACK
EDITOR

Stories by

H. G. WELLS
JULES VERNE
GARRETT P. SERVISS

EXPERIMENTER PUBLISHING COMPANY, NEW YORK, PUBLISHERS OF
RADIO NEWS · SCIENCE & INVENTION · RADIO REVIEW · AMAZING STORIES · RADIO INTERNACIONAL

January

AMAZING STORIES

25 Cents
IN CANADA—THIRTY CENTS

Scientifiction
by

A. Hyatt Verrill

David H. Keller,
M.D.

Miles J. Breuer,
M.D.

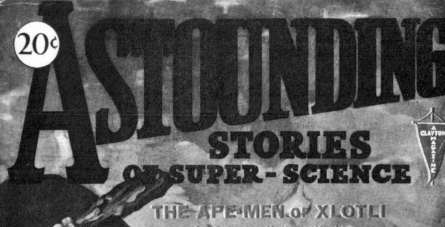

ASTOUNDING

STORIES
of SUPER - SCIENCE

A CLAYTON MAGAZINE

THE APE-MEN of XLOTLI
An Amazing Nether-World Novelette
By DAVID R. SPARKS

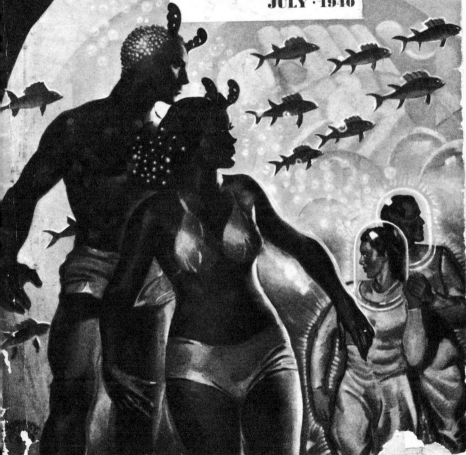

ASTOUNDING

SCIENCE-FICTION
A STREET & SMITH PUBLICATION

JULY · 40

20¢

CRISIS in UTOPIA
BY NORMAN L. KNIGHT

JULY · 1940

15¢

AUGUST

SUPER Science STORIES

A POPULAR PUBLICATION

ccc FEBRUARY 1965 50c 5.

analog

SCIENCE FACT · SCIENCE FICTION

THE MAILMAN COMETH BY **RICK RAPHAEL**

CCC

SCIENCE FICTION

OCTOBER 1974 **75c** 40

.020

analog

SCIENCE FACT

**SPECIAL
VELIKOVSKY
ISSUE**

Isaac
Asimov

Frederic B.
Jueneman

Joe
Haldeman

Harlan
Ellison

This is the kind of awful stuff that still clings to science fiction's reputation, like a mistake you made when you were nine years old that no one will let you forget. When most adults think of science fiction, they think of those dreadful pulp stories. Of course, much of what passes for SF in the movies and on TV is just as bad, and this helps to convince lots of people that science fiction is still miserable trash.

But even in the worst science fiction pulp magazine there was *something* that turned on thoughtful youngsters. Sandwiched in between those lurid covers of frightened lovelies being menaced by giant artichokes were stories and ideas that thrilled the young readers.

The thrill was not sexual. Far from it. Despite the racy covers of those early magazines, science fiction was non-sexual in the sternest Victorian manner. It wasn't until the 1960's that science fiction really discovered sex, and there are still many readers who feel that there's no room in science fiction for anything stronger than an occasional kiss on the cheek.

What excited the pulp readers—youngsters such as Isaac Asimov and Neil Armstrong—was the idea content, the scope, the *grandeur* of science fiction. There is no lesser word to describe what is best in this field: grandeur is where it's at, in science fiction stories.

Rocketships to the Moon, intelligent races on Mars, time travel, death rays, eternal life, the ability to step through solid walls, to fly like a bird, to read men's minds,and to lift mountains with mental power alone—all these concepts appeared in science fiction, even in some of the most godawful prose ever written in the English language. And these ideas struck some of the deepest chords in the human mind. Science fiction told its readers that they could be immortal supermen—gods, if you will. Even though it was only vicarious, the readers loved it.

More than that, science fiction hit its readers squarely in that *urge to know* that we examined in Chapter Two. Young students who were bored with science classes and couldn't stand math or algebra suddenly got turned onto science and the wonders of the universe by reading science fiction. Most of the science in the early pulp stories was dreadfully wrong, but the thrill of sweeping out to the farthest stars and building mighty machines that accomplished titanic feats made thousands of readers realize that there's a lot more to science than memorizing formulas.

Even today, science fiction people talk about the "sense of wonder" that they felt when they first started reading the stuff. The thrill of discovery, whether it's the infinitely small world inside the atom or the infinitely vast cosmos of stars and galaxies, was what lured young readers into the field. And it's been substantiated by many tests and polls of SF readers that they are among the topmost ranks in intelligence. Maybe they didn't do well in class, but once science fiction showed them the beauties and wonder of the universe, they became not only science fiction fans, but worshipers of science and knowledge, as well.

Yet despite this enthusiasm and open-eyed wonder, science fiction was confined to a relatively small number of readers through the entire generation of the 1930's and 40's.

Although Gernsback had no intention of doing so, he had placed science fiction squarely in the ghetto of the pulp magazines. And as any ghetto dweller knows, it's easy to get in and almost impossible to get out. No other kind of publisher would touch science fiction. After all, it was that weird stuff about going to the Moon, wasn't it? Crazy junk!

Since pulp magazines were the only place where a writer could sell science fiction, and the pulps paid very low rates, science fiction failed to attract the best writing talents of the 1930's.

During the economic collapse called the Great Depression and the years of World War II, nearly the whole pulp magazine field died away. Like the dinosaurs, the pulps withered and expired. But not the science fiction magazines. Not all of them, at any rate. They survived, a precious few. And by the end of World War II, they were no longer really pulp magazines anymore.

This survival and improvement of science fiction is sort of like the survival and improvement of our human ancestors through the bitter years of the Ice Age. Science fiction survived the Depression and the war and came out diminished, but much better in quality than it had ever been before.

This evolutionary step forward was due mainly to one single man: John W. Campbell, Jr.

John Campbell became editor of *Astounding Stories* in 1937. At that time he was one of the most prolific and successful writers in the science fiction field. Eventually he gave up writing, because he found something more important to do. He revolutionized science fiction.

His revolution consisted of two simple demands. As editor of *Astounding*, he demanded that his writers produce stories that had good, realistic, sound science in them. And he demanded that his writers produce stories that were good, solid, interesting fiction.

Himself an MIT student and more widely versed in the broad sweep of modern science than most professional scientists, Campbell would not tolerate phony science in a story. Nor would he allow the stiff cardboard figures and standard adventure plots of the earlier pulps. He wanted *ideas* and he wanted strong stories. He got them, largely because he worked long and strenuous hours with writers who were willing to learn how to produce such stories.

The writers that Campbell developed are the Hall of Fame immortals of the field now: Isaac Asimov, Robert A. Heinlein, L. Sprague de Camp, Theodore Sturgeon, Poul Anderson, James Blish, Gordon R. Dickson. The list begins in the late 1930's and goes right through to 1971, when Campbell died unexpectedly of a heart attack.

Over that stretch of 34 years, science fiction became a vital force in American literature. Campbell's influence, long the dominant factor within the science fiction field, is now being felt in the publishing industry as a whole. Science fiction is the only strong remaining market for magazine short stories. There are no other magazines devoted entirely to fiction being published for profit. Most of today's best-selling authors, and all of the so-called "serious" writers of today, are using science fiction themes, ideas, and writing techniques.

Campbell and his writers predicted the world we live in today. They were writing of nuclear weapons and mind-altering drugs back in the 1930's. Science fiction readers knew about these things long before the "experts" in such fields realized they were possible. Science fiction readers were thinking about the impact of globe-spanning communications satellites and rising population pressures and our increasing dependence on a very complex technology that can damage our environment—while their non-SF-reading friends were wearing bobby sox and spending their money on Frankie Laine 45 rpm phonograph records.

In 1960 Campbell converted the name of his magazine from *Astounding* to *Analog*. The new title was more in keeping with science fiction's self-image of a mirror held up to the future, a means of helping everyone to see the possibilities of tomorrow. The name change also confirmed what everyone in the field had known for nearly two decades: The old "gee whiz" days of pulps were dead.

Science fiction began emerging from its ghetto.

But while all this was happening—the vast impact of social upheavals, the incredible power of modern technology unleashed at Hiroshima, the imminence of a new millennium only a generation away, the realization that *change* is an inescapable part of life, the coining of the term "future shock"—while all this was making science fiction the only literature that spoke to the needs of the young reader—the book publishing industry was sleeping away, largely ignoring science fiction.

It's sobering to realize that Isaac Asimov could not get a book of his published in the 1940's. Today, the earnings from his 150-some books have sent the entire boards of directors of many publishing houses on round-the-world vacations. Yet his earliest novels were serialized in *Astounding*, and couldn't find a book publisher. Not until well into the 1950's would any "serious" publisher consider science fiction!

A few publishers were smart enough to realize that there was a market for juvenile science fiction novels, books that would be sold mainly to libraries and read by young people. But even as recently as the early 1960's, what passed for juvenile science fiction was hamstrung by the publishers' insistence that each book must have a 12-year-old hero. So we got a stream of books in which Dick and Jane save the universe.

Gradually this changed. What changed it most was the paperback revolution. When paperback books began appearing everywhere, science fiction quickly became a staple item. At first, this was largely because science fiction writers were hungry and worked cheap. But the publishers quickly found that the younger readers who couldn't afford the price of a hardback book could easily buy paperbacks. And they bought lots of science fiction.

Finally it came home to the hardback publishers that there really were profits to be made in science fiction. By the late 1960's several publishing houses had established science fiction lines, and the quality of the material rose in direct proportion to the prices offered for it.

Today, no matter whether a hardback science fiction novel is tabbed "juvenile," "young adult," or "adult," most of its sales are still to libraries. This means that the material inside the science fiction hardbacks doesn't vary all that much from one age category to another. And the readers of all three categories are apt to be teen-agers and young adults.

Just as the works of Mark Twain and Robert Louis Stevenson can appeal to young and old alike, most of the science fiction hardbacks now being published can be read for fun and profit by anyone old enough to follow the vocabulary.

The blurring of distinctions between adult and juvenile science fiction has also meant that youngsters are reading stories that would have been taboo a few years ago. In the late 1950's, the general rule about juvenile SF was: "no swearing, no drinking, and no sex." You could destroy entire solar systems and remorselessly wipe out billions of people. But no lovemaking!

It was rather ridiculous to have all of space and time for your arena, but not be able to even mention the matters that most young people are aware of and keenly interested in. To keep sex taboo meant keeping the pornographers in business.

Some teachers, librarians, and parents still insist on using their own personal standards of propriety when selecting books for their younger readers —standards that they may not maintain for themselves. They are ignoring the fact that the young readers are often more knowledgeable about sex, war, drugs, and violence than their self-designated protectors.

Many of these young readers like science fiction so much that they try writing it, and often send their stories to *Analog*. While most of them can't be published, it's fascinating to see how much these stories reflect the young writers' awareness of today's problems. Overpopulation, pollution, technologically-aided dictatorships, nuclear or biological war, the impact of discovering other races in space—the problems and opportunities of the future are spelled out in these stories.

These young people know that they're going to live out their lives in the future. They're anxious to learn what it's going to be like. So they write science fiction stories examining parts of the future.

The science fiction readers also share this urge to discover the world of tomorrow. In their attempts to understand the world and make some sense out of it, they turn to science fiction. They are aware, as few adults are, that science and technology are both a problem and a solution.

The way today's young readers and writers perceive themselves and their society is shaped to some extent by what they read. They read science fiction because they are concerned about tomorrow. If they can understand enough about the possibilities that lie ahead, perhaps they can work toward the kind of future they desire.

Until someone actually invents a time machine, science fiction will be the best way we have to examine tomorrow. That's why it's such an exciting field to be in.

The Game

There's a game that's played between science fiction writers and their readers. In fact, it's called The Game.

The writer is free to invent any new scientific discovery or technological breakthrough that he wants to, as long as the readers can't prove that it contradicts what is known today about science. Writers who come up with brilliant new ideas are well-beloved by the readers. But if they can spot a flaw in one of his marvelous new "inventions," they are quick to write him strongly-worded letters that point out where he's fallen down on the job.

A writer like H. G. Wells, for example, could "invent" a serum that makes a man invisible, or a time machine. Wells put just enough explanation into his stories to give the reader a feeling that such an invention might actually work. He never tried to explain how the serum makes a human body transparent, or how the time machine actually works. But he made everything else in the stories so solid and believable that the readers went along with his "impossible" inventions.

If you carefully read *The Invisible Man* or *The Time Machine* today, you'll find that there's not enough explanation of the scientific workings to either prove or disprove Wells' ideas. A physicist might call these inventions flatly impossible, and cite the way human flesh reflects light and how the time machine needs some source of energy to make it work (assuming that it could travel through time, in the first place!).

But a hardened science fiction reader would calmly point out that there's nothing known in science today that proves these ideas are impossible. Unlikely, yes. But not definitely impossible.

As far as the science fiction reader is concerned, Wells passes the test of The Game.

The interplay between science and fiction in SF is not only interesting fun, it creates much of the excitement and value in the science fiction field. The writers are constantly crowding up against the limits of the known facts of science, and pushing farther, into the unknown. It was Arthur C. Clarke, author of *Childhood's End, 2001: A Space Odyssey,* and dozens of other science fiction and science fact books, who coined the phrase:

"The only way to find the limits of the possible is to go beyond them to the impossible."

Science fiction stories do exactly that.

By pushing into areas that are impossible —today—science fiction has excited its readers with a "sense of wonder," and started them *thinking.* Students who are bored with high school physics begin to come alive when they see what all that stuffy science can really accomplish: space ships and robots and computers that actually think!

It's no surprise to SF people that most of the men who've walked on the Moon first got turned on to science by reading science fiction when they were youngsters. And so did most of the people who stayed on the ground at Kennedy Space Flight Center, and in Mission Control in Houston.

Science fiction shows what science and technology can accomplish, rather than how they work. The SF readers see what science can do, and then—if they're really turned on—they go into science classes to see what they can do to add to humankind's storehouse of knowledge.

Science fiction also tries to show the dangers and drawbacks of new scientific discoveries or technological developments. Mary Shelley's classic *Franken-*

stein has often been interpreted as meaning that there are some aspects of knowledge that humans should not poke into. The products of their research—in this case, Dr. Frankenstein's monster—can be dangerous, even lethal. Long before Hiroshima and world ecological crises, science fiction writers were warning of the dangers of unchecked technology.

There's a famous case involving a story in *Astounding* magazine. In 1944, in the midst of World War II and a year before Hiroshima, writer Cleve Cartmill, in a story called *Deadline,* described the basic facts of how to build an atomic bomb. Cartmill and editor John Campbell worked together on the story, drawing their scientific information from papers published in the technical journals before the war. To them, the mechanics of constructing a uranium-fission bomb seemed perfectly obvious.

When the story appeared in print, the FBI swooped down on Campbell's office, looking for spies and demanding that all the copies of that issue of the magazine be taken off the newsstands and impounded. Campbell, who was one of the most persuasive talkers of the Twentieth (or any) Century, pointed out to the grim-faced Federal agents that thousands of people had already seen the magazine, and if it were removed from the newsstands it might convince the readers that Cartmill's story was *very* close to the truth. Instead of protecting the secrets of the Manhattan Project (which had not yet tested its first bomb), the FBI would be advertising to everyone that such a project existed and was aimed at developing nuclear weapons.

Nobody was arrested, and after the war the incident became famous in SF circles, partly because it shows how close to real science a good science fiction story can be.

Although Cartmill was only a few months ahead of reality in that particular story, much of the interest in science fiction comes from stories in which the scientific background is far ahead of current knowledge.

Let's examine the evolution of a science fiction idea, and see how it's influenced by advancing scientific knowledge.

One of the most enduring series of science fiction adventures is Edgar Rice Burroughs' series about Mars. The creator of Tarzan also created a magnificently exotic Mars; peopled with all sorts of strange and wonderful creatures. His hero was a former Virginia cavalry captain, John Carter. The first story in this series, *A Princess of Mars*, was published in 1912.

The scientific background for Burroughs' stories of Barsoom (the Martians' name for their planet) came from the then-current ideas of astronomer Percival Lowell, who saw Mars as a dying world, with thinning air and disappearing water, peopled by an intelligent race who built a planet-spanning system of canals that carried precious water from the polar ice caps to the cities near the equator.

Burroughs set many fine adventures in this kind of Mars. But as time went on, astronomers learned more about Mars and found that Lowell's picture of the planet's environment was far from accurate. Especially, there were no canals and no signs of intelligent life on the Red Planet.

Many SF writers ignored this new knowledge, including Burroughs, who couldn't very well change his Barsoom in mid-series. But the "hard core" science fiction reader would have none of it. Mars isn't like that. Although a writer may set Burroughs' type of florid adventures on another planet, any stories written about Mars had to depict the planet as it really was, to satisfy the rules of The Game.

As astronomical knowledge advanced, the science fiction writers were literally driven out of the solar system. There are no planets in our solar system that are even vaguely like our Earth. Venus was the last hope; perhaps beneath Venus' intriguing clouds the planet was like our own. Many stories were set in a lush, planet-wide jungle on Venus, where dinosaurs still roamed.

The discoveries of the Space Age ended all that. Venus is utterly dry and barren, with a surface temperature hot enough to melt aluminum, and an atmosphere of choking carbon dioxide. No tropical jungles. No place to set an exotic adventure story.

So science fiction writers turned to other solar systems. After all, there are more than a hundred billion stars in our Milky Way galaxy. Many of them are very much like our sun. Surely such stars have Earthlike planets orbiting around them. *That's* the place to set adventure stories.

Please recognize that it's perfectly valid to write exciting stories that take place on Mars or Venus or any other planet, using the conditions there as we know them to exist. Many writers have done exactly that. But when a writer wants to "build" a story on a planet that's like Earth, he's got to go out to the other stars, other solar systems.

Fine. No contradiction with known science. There are undoubtedly millions of Earthlike planets orbiting other stars.

But—how do we get there from here? And if we need to have our hero travel back and forth between Earth and Planet Exotica, how can this be done? The distances between the stars are so vast that it would take centuries, even thousands of years, to go from one star to another. This is known scientific fact.

Faced with this celestial roadblock, science fiction writers dipped into their imaginations and came up with *space warps*. All right, they admitted, if you tried to fly from one star to another in normal space, where you're limited to the speed of light as the absolute top speed attainable (fact), it will take many lifetimes to get where you want to go. But if we can devise a space warp, and enter *hyperspace* where the speed of light is not a limiting factor, then we can go anywhere as fast as we want to.

Physicists and astronomers winced at the idea. There are no space warps, they insisted. And hyperspace is at best an abstraction invented by mathematical theorists, not a physical reality.

But the science fiction readers smiled and nodded. The ideas of space warps and hyperspace didn't violate the rules of The Game. Just because they haven't been discovered doesn't mean that they can't exist. Nobody could prove they were impossible.

And, in fact, astronomers and physicists over the past five years or so have started talking about ways to travel faster than light. Perhaps they were stimulated by reading science fiction. Perhaps not. But nowadays, at many scientific conferences, there are serious discussions of *tachyons*—hypothetical particles that move faster than light—and of the gravitational pits called *black holes*, the residue from a collapsing star, that warps not only space but time.

Hamlet told Horatio that there are more things in heaven and Earth than the philosophers dreamed of. Science fiction writers and readers hold that as a basic tenet of faith.

There are some cases where a new scientific idea is espoused in science fiction long before the scientists themselves begin to believe it. In fact, I stumbled across such an idea myself, mainly by accident.

Back in the early 1960's, I was writing a series of articles on the possibilities of life existing on other worlds for a science fiction magazine. One of the key points in my chain of reasoning was the question of whether or not planets form naturally around most stars, and if they do, whether or not they contain in their make-up the necessary chemical ingredients from which living creatures can be produced.

In other words, could I show that most stars have planets orbiting around them, and that these planets have the chemical building-blocks necessary for the creation of life? The evidence on hand seemed to indicate that the answer to both questions was *yes*.

Not only that. It occurred to me that the known sequence of events leading to the formation of a star and its planets might also lead to the formation of the chemical compounds necessary for life. Stars are formed in swirling clouds of interstellar gas. As they begin to condense and take shape and glow, smaller condensations in the gas around them form planets. Almost all of the material in these clouds consists of the two simplest, lightest elements of the universe: hydrogen and helium. But there is a smattering of other elements including oxygen, carbon, and nitrogen.

So, I speculated to myself, perhaps there could be conditions in the early stages of a new solar system's formation where the basic chemical ingredients of life are put together out of this interstellar cloud's contents. The line I actually wrote in the magazine was merely: "Space is too cold for biochemical reactions, except for the first primitive steps of chemical evolution . . ."

That was published in November, 1962. Within a few years, radio astronomers were discovering complex molecules of carbon compounds, ammonia, water vapor, and other building-blocks of life in interstellar space. Where? In the swirling clouds where new stars and new solar systems are being created!

I started kicking myself for not following up on my own idea and at least getting a little credit for it. Then I thought of Arthur C. Clarke, who in 1945 wrote an article that showed that artificial satellites would make ideal relay stations for worldwide radio, telephone, and television transmissions. When the first communications satellites went into orbit, 20 years later, Clarke wrote a glum essay titled, *How I Lost a Billion Dollars in my Spare Time.*

Science fiction is sprinkled with these poignant little incidents. When Mariner 4 took the first close-up photos of Mars on July 14, 1965, astronomers all over the world were astounded to see that the Red Planet is almost as crater-pocked as the Moon. Yet

George W. Harper had predicted this in an article published in May, 1963, in *Analog*.

Of course, science fiction writers aren't always right and aren't always ahead of the facts.

There's the famous case of Apollo 11. No one has counted how many stories have been written about the first landing on the Moon. Cyrano de Bergerac started the business more than three centuries ago. H. G. Wells, Robert Heinlein, Isaac Asimov and just about every writer who's ever tried his hand at science fiction have all done stories about the first lunar landing.

Not one of them foresaw the fact that there would be live TV transmission from the Moon.

There's a reason for this. Not an excuse, but a reason. By the time Project Apollo got seriously underway, stories about landing on the Moon were old hat in science fiction. There seems to be an unwritten corollary to The Game that states: "If you can read about it in the newspapers, it's no longer interesting in science fiction."

Most of the modern stories about reaching the Moon were written prior to 1950. When Robert Heinlein's movie, *Destination Moon*, woke up the entire world to the fact that we could actually accomplish this feat, Moon-flight stories disappeared from the science fiction field almost entirely. In 1950, television was a boisterous new toy. None of the writers working prior to that time thought about TV's impact hard enough to realize that by the time men actually did touch down on the Moon, everyone in the U.S. would have a TV set and they'd all want to see the historic moment for themselves.

Science fiction writers are human.

Not only are they human, but they write about human beings. It's easy to get the impression, if you haven't read much SF, that the stories are mainly about machines, or strange places, or scientific research. They're not. The robots and space ships and exotic new worlds are merely the background. They're the *science* in science fiction. There's also the *fiction* to consider.

Science fiction stories try to show how human beings are affected by new scientific discoveries or technological inventions. In fact, a workable definition of science fiction could be: "Stories in which the characters are affected by some aspect of science or technology."

If you can take the science or technology out of a story and still have a story that makes sense, then it's not really science fiction. It may be a perfectly good story, but the chances are that it will work better as a contemporary tale, rather than SF.

For example, consider Jules Verne's classic, *Twenty Thousand Leagues Under the Sea*. Its basic premise is simple. Captain Nemo is bent on stopping nations from making war. He wants to destroy the war-making capabilities of the great powers, and thus bring peace to the world. To do this, Nemo builds and operates the submarine Nautilus. He lives in an underwater world and terrifies the world by sinking war ships.

Take away the submarine, the trappings of Nemo's underwater world, and the story collapses. Yet Verne was not writing about how wonderful submarines are. He was telling his readers that the war machinery of their day was evil, destructive, and would lead humanity to ruin. Few listened to that message. World War I eventually exploded, and Verne's world was forever destroyed.

Incidentally, although Verne "invented" many marvels for Captain Nemo, he is given credit for one invention that never appeared in the story. Many people assume that the Nautilus was equipped with a periscope. There is no mention of a periscope in Verne's novel.

The human element. The interaction of human beings, with all their emotions and drives, with new science and technology. That's science fiction.

It's not merely predicting new inventions. It's not merely showing strange and wonderful places. The real impact of science fiction comes from showing how humans react to the worlds of the future. That's the *real* game of science fiction.

Take Robert Heinlein's story, *The Roads Must Roll*. Published in June 1940, this story deals with inter-continental highways and their impact on society. Heinlein's roads are actually huge conveyor belts. The roads *do* roll, and you can step aboard them just as you step aboard a moving sidewalk at an airport.

Except for that dramatic technical difference, Heinlein's roads are very much like the network of interstate highways that have been built across the U.S. over the past 20 years. And Heinlein was able to foresee what the effects of such a road system would be: people moving away from the major cities into the previously-unoccupied suburbs and countryside. The explosion of suburbia over the past two decades has been caused in part by the network of superhighways that allows millions of people to drive in and out of the central city each day.

But Heinlein's vision went deeper than that. What happens if the roads *don't* roll? In his story, the technicians and engineers who control the roads go out on strike. The roads stop; the nation is paralyzed.

In the real world of the 1970's, we see situations where immense traffic jams temporarily prevent the roads from "rolling." And strikes by truckdrivers or railroad men or airline personnel can cause all sorts of tangles and grief.

What was Heinlein trying to tell us? First, he was trying to write an exciting, interesting story. The underlying message of the story, though, is that the more complicated our society becomes, the more it depends on technology, the easier it will be for a small group of people to paralyze it. If more people had gotten that message into their skulls in the 1940's, perhaps our transportation systems would have been better designed.

In science fiction, the characters aren't always human beings. There are robots, aliens from other worlds, or intelligent dolphins. A story of mine once had a gorilla as one of its main characters; his brain had been altered by scientists to the point where he was as intelligent as a six-year-old human child. But he was still a 400-pound black mountain gorilla. Gentle, but very strong.

The point is, the characters don't have to look like humans in a science fiction story. But they usually must behave like humans, especially if they're the major characters in the story.

This stems from a very basic factor in the art of storytelling. The reader automatically identifies himself with the main character of the story. If the main character is Robin Hood, the reader sees *himself* bounding through Sherwood Forest two jumps ahead of the Sheriff of Nottingham. If the main character is a robot, the reader unconsciously wants to know what it's like to be a robot, how the world looks from inside the robot's brain. If the robot doesn't behave like a human, the reader tends to feel left out of the story, and usually won't react to it too well.

There are plenty of science fiction stories in which there are robots that are minor characters, or even just part of the background. That kind of robot can be as mechanical and dull as a dishwashing machine. But when Isaac Asimov started writing stories in which robots were central characters, the robots had to be quite human, and subject to the same problems of behavior as we are.

So Asimov hit on the Three Laws of Robotics, which are basic rules of behavior that are programmed into the brains of every robot in Asimov's stories. They are:

1. A robot may not injure a human being, or, through inaction, allow a human being to come to harm.

2. A robot must obey the orders given it by human beings except where such orders would conflict with the First Law.

3. A robot must protect its own existence as long as such protection does not conflict with the First and Second Laws.

Asimov had enormous fun writing dozens of stories in which he deliberately set up conflicts among the Laws, and gave the robots problems that looked unsolvable. The readers had even more fun trying to figure out how he would solve them, and then seeing how it was actually done, usually on the very last page.

But think about those Laws for a moment. They make pretty good sense for people, don't they? The First Law sounds almost like the Golden Rule of, "Do unto others as you would have them do unto you." The Second Law sounds very much like the attitude parents have toward children. And the Third Law is a simple statement of self-preservation, modified by the higher ideal of sacrifice.

The point is, Asimov wasn't writing only about futuristic machines. He was writing about us, about what it means to be human, to be alive, to have to live by certain kinds of rules and to experience the conflicts between self-desire and socially-acceptable behavior.

Beneath all the wonderful discoveries and shining new machines, science fiction is really talking about the things that all fiction speaks of: the essence of humanity. But science fiction can and does bring out one facet of the human experience in a way that's stronger and more consistent than any other form of fiction can do.

That is the very basic concept of *change*. The scientific and technological marvels in science fiction stories are actually ways of showing the reader that the world is constantly changing. This is what lifts SF out of the here-and-now. But even more importantly, science fiction often shows that even though change is inevitable, human actions can influence, shape, mold the very process of change itself. We can literally make our own future. We can make changes that are beneficial and worthwhile. Or at the very least, we can *try*.

Basic human nature doesn't change, not even in science fiction stories. But the world that we build for ourselves is enormously affected by science and technology. Science fiction tries to show this and points out that there are still more and bigger changes to come.

There's an old motto of the Navy Construction Battalions, the fabled Seabees: "The impossible we do right away; the miraculous takes a little time."

Science fiction has dealt with many ideas and inventions that were once considered impossible by most people—including most scientists.

We've already seen that stories were written about atomic bombs long before Hiroshima. But decades earlier, science fiction writers were dealing with the peaceful uses of energy that's tapped from Einstein's famous formula, $E = mc^2$. The current problems of the safety and wisdom of using nuclear energy were in science fiction more than a generation ago.

Of course, science fiction writers have been credited with "predicting" that man would go to the Moon. Very few people understand, however, how much science fiction writers did to help make their stories become reality.

In the first place, science fiction stories about space flight helped to stimulate the imaginations of young readers in the decades of the 1920's, 30's, and 40's. Men such as Wernher Von Braun became interested in space flight through encountering science fiction as teenagers.

Others, such as Arthur C. Clarke, who were respected engineers as well as writers, actually influenced some scientists and engineers to push for space flight programs in the U.S. and Great Britain.

While most people were poking fun at the idea of flying in space, science fiction stories were showing how it could be done. Other stories were dealing with drugs or electronic devices that could control a person's mind. Again, even serious scientists laughed—until LSD and biofeedback machines and "brainwashing" became everyday words.

Stories are being written today about genetic manipulation, the ability to deliberately alter the genes of unborn babies in order to change their physical or mental traits. Most people think of this as a far-off possibility, if they think of it at all. Yet the biochemists and geneticists, who have already produced "test tube" human babies are trying desperately to get the attention of the public focused on the dangers—and the marvelous opportunities—that their work is presenting to us.

The impossible is here with us today. The miraculous will come, in time.

We will find, somewhere in the vast depths of space, other intelligent creatures. There are civilizations built by races that are more intelligent and far older than we. What will we do when we find them—or they find us? Science fiction writers are exploring the possibilities in dozens of stories each year.

We will someday learn to build spacecraft that can go to the stars. Or perhaps we'll learn to cross those vast interstellar distances in some other way —through space warping, black holes, or by telepathic power. We will greatly increase our life spans and reach toward true immortality. What will happen to the human race then?

If the physical universe of stars and space has any limits to it, scientists have not yet found those limits. Nor has any human being found a limit to the universe inside the human mind.

In science fiction, we try to explore both those limitless domains, using what's known about the world that science can explain to us, and what's known about the human spirit. Science fiction writers and readers play their Game as fairly as they can. But they always remember that the true objective of The Game is to produce solid stories, based on scientific knowledge. Stories that make you *think*.

The Hunters

CHAPTER FIVE

The first story that most school children hear about scientists is usually the story of Archimedes.

The tale is told of how this Greek philosopher-engineer discovered the principle of buoyancy, or water displacement, when he sat in a bathtub brimful of water and some of the water spilled over the tub's edge. He immediately realized that the amount of water his body displaced was an accurate measure of his own body's mass, or weight. And just as quickly, he leaped out of the tub and went racing through the streets of ancient Syracuse, naked and dripping, shouting, "Eureka!" (Which means, "I've found it!" *It*, in this case, being the principle of water displacement.)

So the first image that most school children get of a scientist is a picture of some nut running naked and screaming through the city streets.

Later on, as students enter high school and take science courses, their picture of science and scientists apparently changes drastically. Surveys in the U.S. and Great Britain have shown that most teen-aged students think of scientists as being very intelligent, cold, lacking in humor, unfriendly, extremely careful in everything they do—in short, they see scientists as the kind of people who'd rather spend Saturday night peering into a microscope, rather than going out to a dance.

Perhaps the teen-agers get this impression from their high school science teachers, who are—after all—the closest thing to a real scientist that most teens have had a chance to see. Or it might be garnered from the science courses themselves, where too much emphasis is put on getting exactly the right answer to questions that are trivial (such as the mechanical advantage of a set of pulleys) and not enough attention is placed on appreciating the broad understandings and simple beauties of science.

Most likely, though, the students get their sour impressions of scientists from watching movies and TV. In all too many shows, scientists are presented as fuzzy-headed, rumple-clothed, nearsighted old men who might be terrific in a laboratory but are miserable failures anywhere else. The absent-minded professor, who can whip together a brew that will turn a mouse into a lion, yet can't stand up to his henpecking wife, is a stock character in countless old movies.

But there's a much more dangerous kind of "scientist" also depicted in movies and on TV. This is the ruthless, power-mad megalomaniac who tampers with forces that ought to be left alone, so that his dreadful knowledge can be used to rule the world.

The brilliant, cold-blooded, ruthless scientist is not a new invention of Hollywood. Goethe wrote about him in *Faust*, in 1832. A dozen years earlier, Mary Wollstonecraft Shelley had written of him in *Frankenstein*. And two centuries before that, Shakespeare had depicted a powerful wizard in *The Tempest* who was transformed in the 1950's into a knowledge-hungry scientist who unwittingly threatened to destroy the entire human race, when Shakespeare's play was used as the basis for the science fiction movie, *Forbidden Planet*.

Which of these two images of the scientist is closer to the truth? Are scientists eccentric crackpots who are apt to go running naked through the streets when they get excited over a new idea? Or are they cold-blooded Dr. Strangeloves, who can contemplate all-out nuclear war with a grim smile on their lips?

Neither, of course. But of the two types, scientists tend much more toward the Archimedes type than the Dr. Strangelove.

Consider the *real* lessons of the Archimedes story. First, the tale shows that a man can get so emotionally involved in the world of ideas, so excited about a new intellectual discovery, that he forgets where he is and reacts purely emotionally. (Besides, what most students—and teachers—fail to realize is that public nudity was not at all shocking to the ancient Greeks.)

Moreover, the truly marvelous part of the story is Archimedes' flash of intuition. He stepped into the tub and sat down. The water spilled over the tub's edge. Immediately something clicked in the man's brain. He recognized in a flash that he could weigh all sorts of objects by immersing them in water and measuring the amount of water they displaced.

He didn't spend hours poring over notes. He didn't even bother to check out the basic idea. In a lightning burst of intuition, *he knew!* And he reacted accordingly.

For all of human existence, except the most recent times, our ancestors have been hunters. Since the hominids came down out of the trees, hunting has been our way of life. The past hundred centuries of agriculture have changed our society and brought most humans into cities, but they have not changed our brains and our bodies. We are built, shaped, and trained emotionally and mentally for the hunting life.

Scientists are hunters. Their quarry may lie out among the stars, or deep in the nucleus of atoms, or within the intricate neural connections of the human brain. And they may catch their quarry only after long years of patient, careful stalking—or in a sudden burst of insight, as Archimedes did.

But it is the thrill of the hunt that makes science the exciting pursuit that it is.

And these hunters of the mind need more than patience and skill, more than tools and weapons. Their most important need is *imagination.* For new discoveries can only be made by those whose minds are open to recognize something—some idea, relationship, piece of evidence—that has never been seen before. Without imagination, science becomes little more than ritual. With imagination, scientists have been able to challenge the universe.

Science depends on steady, careful, tedious, day-to-day research. But every new leap forward in scientific understanding began in a flash of imagination, a sudden burst of intuition, a hunch.

As we saw in Chapter Two, Copernicus created the theory that the sun, rather than the Earth, is at the center of the solar system. He was so timid about his idea, so fearful of the reaction it would stir up, that he didn't allow his theory to be published until he was on his deathbed. And it took more than three generations of argument, research, and discovery to prove the heliocentric theory is correct.

The basic lesson of Copernicus was to show that our Earth is not a special and unique place, the center of the universe. Yet it took nearly a century before the Copernican idea was accepted by the leading thinkers of Europe. Ever since that time, astronomers and cosmologists have been trying to puzzle out exactly where our planet fits into the scheme of the universe, and whether or not there are other worlds like ours in space, with life on them—possibly even intelligent life.

Copernicus' *heliocentric* (sun-centered) theory was first published in 1543. The argument over his idea raged hotly throughout Europe. In those days, scientific ideas were considered to be a challenge to the authority of both Church and state. Martin Luther called Copernicus a lunatic for trying to make people think that the Earth moved around the sun. Giordano Bruno, an Italian monk, was burned at the stake in 1600 for refusing to accept the teaching of his Roman Catholic superiors that the Earth was flat and unmoving and at the center of the universe.

But in 1609 Galileo Galilei produced unquestionable proof of the Copernican concept, when he first turned a crude telescope to the night sky.

He saw a solar system that was Copernican, not Earth-centered, as we saw in Chapter Two. Although Galileo was forced to recant his views by the still-powerful Roman Catholic Church, or face life imprisonment, his discoveries eventually convinced even the Church officials that Copernicus was right. The Earth is not the center of the universe. Our planet, and all the planets of the solar system, revolve around the sun.

More than that. Galileo's telescope showed that there are myriads more stars in the sky than can be seen with the unaided eye. And that softly-glowing band of light called the Milky Way resolves itself, in the telescope, into countless teeming clouds of stars.

The telescope became the prime instrument of astronomers over the next centuries, and much skill and devotion was spent in building constantly bigger and better instruments. The more powerful the telescope, the more stars it revealed to the astronomers.

It became apparent that our sun is just one of billions upon billions of stars that make up the great congregation called the Milky Way. Then the question arose: Where are we located within the Milky Way?

By the beginning of the Twentieth Century, astronomers had found an answer. But they didn't like it.

After checking carefully in all directions of the sky and measuring the numbers of stars in every direction around us, the astronomers came to a very disturbing conclusion. The Milky Way seemed to be shaped more-or-less like a pie plate: round and flattened. And our solar system was apparently smack in the middle of it!

In other words, we appeared to be at the center of the universe.

This made the astronomers very uneasy, for the lesson of Copernicus was that our situation in the universe is not unique; we are not the center of things.

It was a young American astronomer, Harlow Shapley (1885-1972) who changed the picture. He proved that the conclusions reached by all the most prominent astronomers of the age were wrong. This is an important lesson in science: Any young pup can upset the conclusions of all the top dogs—if he has the proof. There are no sacred ideas in science that can't be overthrown.

Shapley showed that our Milky Way is surrounded by a "halo" of huge star clusters. These globular-shaped clusters contain hundreds of thousands of stars each. About one-third of all the globular clusters we can see are concentrated in a two-percent area of our sky, in the region marked out by the constellation Sagittarius.

Shapley guessed—there's no better word—that the clusters are actually spread evenly around the Milky Way's center, and they seemed to be grouped off in one end of the sky because we are actually far away from that center.

In a famous debate before the National Academy of Sciences in Washington on April 26, 1920, Shapley argued his case against Heber D. Curtis (1872-1942) of the Lick Observatory. They argued two points: first, whether or not our solar system is at the center of the Milky Way; and second, whether or not the Milky Way encompassed the entire universe, or was merely one large "island" of stars among many such "islands."

Curtis argued that our solar system is at the Milky Way's center, and the Milky Way is just one galaxy of stars in a universe populated by many such "island" galaxies. Shapley claimed that the solar system is off to one side of the Milky Way, and the Milky Way *is* the whole universe.

The argument wasn't settled that night; not for many years, in fact. Both men were partly right and partly wrong. Shapley was right about our location in the Milky Way; we're actually some 30,000 light-years from its center. But, as the work of Edwin P. Hubble (1899-1953) and others proved later in the 1920's, our Milky Way is only one galaxy in a universe filled with hundreds of billions of galaxies.

From being the center of the universe to being a tiny planet circling a very average star, far off from the center of a galaxy that's merely one of a hundred billion or so galaxies—we've come a long way, baby.

While our location in the universe was being puzzled out, other astronomers were trying to determine if we are unique in another sense: Is the sun the only star that has planets orbiting around it?

Even the stars closest to our solar system are so far off that any planets orbiting around them would be invisible to the most powerful telescopes on Earth. However, astronomers are nothing if not ingenious, and they have painstakingly measured the motions of the nearer stars to see if they can detect the miniscule gravitational pulls that planets might exert on their parent stars.

Several of the nearest stars do show tiny wobbles in their courses through space that could be caused by the gravitational influences of planets.

Bringing together pieces of evidence such as this, with many other clues and ideas, astronomers and cosmologists have now deduced that many stars form with planetary systems around them. Our solar system is not unique. The formation of planets is just as natural as the birth of stars, and new stars are being created deep in interstellar space all the time.

On our particular planet, the conditions of temperature and chemical composition were right for the formation of huge bodies of liquid water. Earth is the only planet in the solar system where such conditions prevail. In those ancient seas various chemicals came together to form the first, simplest living things—long-chain molecules that could reproduce themselves and feed on the simpler molecules that floated in those warm seas. One such molecule —called by biochemists deoxyribonucleic acid (DNA) —is at the heart of every cell in every living creature on Earth. Including you and me. DNA is the basic chemical ingredient of life on Earth.

Although our planet may not be located at the center of the vast universe, we are the only planet in the solar system that bears intelligent life. There may be life forms on Mars or even Jupiter. But apparently there is no intelligent life elsewhere in the solar system. But beyond?

If, as the astronomers now believe, stars tend to have planets circling around them as a natural result of the way they're created, then there must be many planets like Earth in the universe. If that's true, the biologists and biochemists tell us, then the chances are that on such planets life will arise, just as it arose here. Given sufficient time, such life could develop intelligence, just as we have. Nothing unique about it at all.

To some people, it's been a crushing blow to the ego to find that we are not the center of the universe, that we are located far from the center of our galaxy, living on a tiny planet that orbits a quite average type of star. Yet it is a thrilling, magnificent accomplishment of the human mind and spirit to seek out this knowledge, and find it. We may live on a tiny planet, true enough, but our minds are great enough to encompass this whole vast universe of which we are a part.

Much the same emotional reaction comes about when people try to determine how the human race came to be. What are our origins? When and how did we arise on planet Earth?

In the beginning, men who tried to puzzle out how the human race fits into the scheme of life, and how we came into being, had nothing to go on except their imaginations. Every tribe, every society, every culture has its mythology concerning the origins of humankind. Like the earliest ideas in astronomy, these mythological explanations always placed man at the center of the universe, the most important creature in the world.

Obviously we are the most important creatures on Earth. To ourselves. And it is easy to see that we are the dominant creatures of this planet. We have driven many other animal species into extinction. We are now unthinkingly pushing most of the remaining large animal species into oblivion: the whale, the gorilla, the bison, eagle, lion . . . the list fills pages.

But it was not always so.

The *scientific* search for human origins has shown that our ancient ancestors began as small, almost insignificant tree dwelling mammals, as we saw in Chapter One.

How do we know this is true? What is the evidence for humankind's evolution?

The start of this particular hunt began more than a century ago. And, as with most hunting expeditions, imagination and stubbornness played as vital a role as the meticulous search for evidence.

Several times in the early Nineteenth Century, workmen digging in caves or quarries uncovered strange-looking bones and skulls. Usually they were tossed away, with no attention paid to them. On a couple of occasions, unusual bones were delivered to the nearest school or scientific society, where they were put on a shelf to gather dust and forgotten.

At that time, most Europeans and Americans firmly believed the Biblical account of humanity's origins and early history. Adam and Eve were the first humans, and they were driven from the Garden of Eden by disobeying the rules of God. Later, after humankind had grown greatly in both numbers and wickedness, God sent a flood that wiped out everybody except the family of Noah.

In 1856, quarry workers digging in a little valley called the Neanderthal, near Düsseldorf in Germany, found some weird-looking bones. At first they thought that the bones belonged to some animal, and tossed them aside. But the owner of the quarry, a Mr. Beckershoff, found them and became curious about them.

Driven by his urge to know, Beckershoff gathered up some arm and thigh bones, the top of a strange-looking skull, and part of a pelvis. He took them to J. C. Fuhlrott, who was a teacher in the nearby town of Elberfield and a founder of the Natural Science Society there.

Fuhlrott immediately recognized that these bones had become fossilized. That is, the original biological material of the bones had been replaced, over a staggeringly long period of time, by mineral material. A fossil is a bone or other once-living item that has literally "turned into stone."

He concluded that the bones were very ancient, most likely "antediluvian," meaning older than the Biblical flood. Perhaps, Fuhlrott reasoned, they were the bones of a man who was drowned in the flood.

At this time, 1856, geologists had only the first glimmerings of knowledge about the Ice Age and the earlier history of the Earth. The whole concept of evolution—the gradual change in plant and animal species that produces new species in time—was still quite new and being heatedly debated by scientists throughout Europe.

Without realizing it, Fuhlrott had identified what later became known as Neanderthal Man, the first of our ancient ancestors to be discovered.

Even while the quarrymen were unearthing Neanderthal Man's fossilized bones, in England the naturalist Charles Darwin (1809-1882) was working on his monumental treatise, *Origin of the Species.* As naturalist aboard the scientific research vessel, H.M.S. *Beagle* from 1831 to 1836, Darwin had seen variations in plant and animal life all around the world. He returned to England with the basic ideas of natural selection and evolution in his mind.

Darwin had come to the conclusion that living creatures change and adapt to their varying environments, over the course of long ages of time. *Natural selection,* as he saw it, is a process whereby creatures that are well-adapted to their environment survive and have offspring. Those that are not well-adapted die away. Over many, many generations, species will be subjected to *mutations,* which are changes in its basic genetic make-up. Most of these mutations are either unnoticeable or harmful, and cause the species to die off. But some mutations are helpful, and allow the species to survive better in its environment, or even to grow into a new and different environment and flourish there.

In Chapter Two we saw that our primordial ancestors evolved from tree shrews to science fiction writers. Some of the helpful mutations along that evolutionary trail included the development of a flexible hand with a strong, opposable thumb; binocular stereo and color vision; legs and feet that became adapted for walking erect; and a large, complex brain. Some of the physical traits that we lost along the way include tail, claws, fangs, most body hair, grasping feet, and a set of muscles that would make Tarzan look puny.

But we digress.

In 1856 Darwin's book was still three years from being published. A furor broke out over the discovery of Neanderthal Man. Careful researcher that he was, Darwin didn't rush into publication with his ideas. Although his work showed considerable imagination, he still spent 23 years gathering evidence for evolution and natural selection before revealing his ideas to the world.

Meanwhile, all of Europe's naturalists, scientists, religious leaders, and everyone else who could read (and quite a few who couldn't) got into a furious brawl about the Neanderthal fossils.

Many people refused to believe that the fossils could be so ancient. They are the bones of an ordinary human being, it was said. One thinker concluded that the bones were those of a Mongol soldier from the Russian army that had fought Napoleon in 1814. When asked why the skull looked so unlike an ordinary human skull—it had very thick walls, was flatter and longer than our skulls, and had massive bone ridges over the eyes and practically no chin—the answers were ludicrous: The Mongol soldier was wounded, and the pain made him pucker his brows as he crawled into the cave to die. Try puckering your brows for as long as you like and see if it changes the bony structure of your skull!

Eventually, as more and more evidence began to pour in from diggings all across Europe and the Near East, it was grudgingly admitted by most thinking men that there had been an ancient "ape man." When Darwin's *Origin of the Species* was finally published, his concept of evolution became as vital to the biological sciences as Copernicus' heliocentric concept was to astronomy. With one clear, central idea—evolution—Darwin provided a basic structure onto which the entire background and history of human origins and development could be placed into an organized and logical order.

The search for humanity's origins goes on, although the major facts of the story are now well-known. We are the descendants of tree dwelling animals who evolved many different species over the 70-some million years since the dinosaurs disappeared. There is no "missing link" between us and the apes, because we are not evolved from the apes.

Apes and humans developed side-by-side over the past few million years; we are cousins, not father-and-son.

In general, the course of the evolutionary trail that leads to *Homo sapiens sapiens* is now quite clear, even though there are still gaps in the fossil record and many interesting questions to answer. The exact mechanisms, down on the genetic and molecular level, of how creatures change and mutate from one species to another is still somewhere between a miracle and mystery. But the basic process is understood, thanks largely to hunter-scientists such as Francis Crick and James Watson, who unravelled the structure of deoxyribonucleic acid (DNA), the molecule that forms the basic genetic material of all the living creatures on Earth.

Just as in the centuries-long hunt for Earth's place in the universe, many dedicated scientists have participated in the hunt for man's origins. Instead of peering into the skies, these men have tramped out into the wildest places, eyes focused on the ground, where fossils are buried.

Mary and Louis Leakey are probably the most famous fossil hunters of our times. They spent their lives searching for the remains of our ancestors, starting with a hunt they undertook in 1924 for dinosaur bones. They soon found that human fossils are much more interesting and, despite great hardships and personal sacrifices, they trekked through many parts of Africa in search of our long-dead ancestors. It was the Leakey's who discovered such extensive remains of *Homo erectus* in Olduvai Gorge, a site where our ancestors had made their hunting camps for perhaps more than a million years. Louis Leakey died in 1973, at an age of 70. His wife and son Richard are carrying on the work.

In one scientific field after another, we find the same pattern: curiosity starts the hunters on the trail; in the beginning there is usually so little to go on that they "follow their noses" and use imagination and intuition as their guides; they form a theory, then search for evidence to either confirm the theory or knock it down. Finally, if the theory is confirmed, it will suggest new ideas, new places to seek evidence, the beginnings of new hunts. And always these hunts take generations. Like most human endeavors, science is the work of many humans cooperating with each other—even though they may live centuries apart, in different ends of the world.

This is the way new knowledge is uncovered. This is the hunt that we call science.

Benjamin Franklin (1706–1790) stands out in a thunderstorm flying a kite, because he has a hunch that electricity and lightning are one and the same thing. James Clerk Maxwell (1831–1879) of Scotland, working with little more than a pencil and paper, theorizes that electricity and magnetism are two parts of the same phenomenon: electromagnetism. Moreover, with virtually no evidence to back up his idea, Maxwell jumps to the conclusion that *light* is a form of electromagnetic wave, and there are many other forms of such waves, invisible to our eyes.

Nine years after Maxwell's death, the German physicist Heinrich Hertz (1857–1894) discovers the first of these "invisible waves." At first they're called *Hertzian waves;* later they get to be known as *radio waves.* Guglielmo Marconi (1874–1937) transmits a radio signal across the Atlantic Ocean in 1901, and the electronics industry is born.

But more than that. Scientists are surprised that radio signals don't waft off into space, but instead seem to be able to curve around the Earth's horizon. They find that there are layers of electrically-charged gases high up in the Earth's atmosphere that reflect certain kinds of radio waves. This layer of the atmosphere becomes known as the *ionosphere.*

From a wild kite flight to the birth of a new industry and a fundamental discovery about the nature of our planet, in two centuries and eight generations of researchers.

One of the men who studied the electrically-charged gases (or *plasmas,* as physicists call them) was Irving Langmuir (1881–1957). He received a

Nobel Prize for his research in 1932. In the late 1940's, at an age when most men are ready to retire, Langmuir started an entirely new career—in weather modification.

Langmuir's work in cloud seeding brought him little but frustration and trouble. People blamed him for floods. And droughts. The government decided that cloud-seeding operations weren't worthwhile. He died a very disappointed man.

Yet the hunt for intelligent control of the weather goes on today. Weather modification research is proceeding in dozens of nations. Crops and forests are being protected from natural disasters, such as hailstorms and lightning, through cloud-seeding techniques. Giant hurricanes have been altered by following the ideas that Langmuir originated.

The hunt goes on.

Of all the people in our civilized world, it is the scientists who come the closest to the spirit of the ancient hunter that lies inside all of us. This is why science is so exhilarating to its practitioners; this is why scientists can be such exciting and excitable people.

They may not run naked and shouting through the streets anymore, but the most satisfying word a scientist can utter is still, "Eureka!"

To Boldly Go!!!

CHAPTER SIX

Date: December 1968. *Place:* Belmont, Massachusetts, a residential suburb of Boston. *Occasion:* a Sunday afternoon meeting of the New England Science Fiction Association.

We stopped the regular business of the meeting to watch the first television transmission from Apollo 8. This forerunner of the lunar landing mission was on its way to a flight around the Moon, carrying astronauts Frank Borman, James Lovell, and William Anders. A few evenings later they were to make an historic Christmas Eve television broadcast from within a few hundred kilometers of the Moon's barren surface.

But at this moment they were on their way to the Moon, about 50,000 kilometers or so from Earth, setting a new distance record with every millimeter they travelled, for no human had ever ventured so far from our homeworld before.

As they cheerfully showed what life aboard an Apollo capsule was like, somebody in that awe-struck group in Belmont muttered a line from the then-popular TV show, *Star Trek:*

"To boldly go where no man has gone before."

Borman, Lovell, and Anders were breaking new ground in humankind's age-old urge to explore. And it occurred to me at that dramatic moment that science fiction does exactly the same thing, when it's good: It takes the reader on a bold journey of imagination into regions of thought that haven't previously been explored.

Of course, science itself does this, too. From space probes to electron microscopes, scientific research is aimed at uncovering new knowledge. Researchers explore where no one has gone before.

The similarities and differences between the scientific approach and the science fiction approach to exploring new territory can be shown by considering one of the gravest problems facing the human race today: The inevitable moment when we have used up all the natural resources of our world.

In 1972, a very controversial book was published. Titled *The Limits to Growth,* it was a study of the world's future done by a team of scientists from the Massachusetts Institute of Technology (MIT). They used computer "models" of the future of our society, and found that there's a planet-wide disaster facing us unless we sharply limit the growth of our population and consumption of natural resources.

The MIT group worked out a technique for simulating certain aspects of the world's social and economic behavior. Then the computer showed how these different factors are interrelated and how they affect one another. For example, the computer model could show how world population grows when the death rate is kept low and the birth rate stays high; how consumption of natural resources is affected by increasing population; how growing industrial output leads to growing pollution. Putting these and many other factors together, the study showed that total disaster is awaiting the human race within another 70 to 100 years.

According to the computer's model of the world's future, if we don't change our present style of growth-oriented society, and change it drastically and *soon,* we will quickly use up all of the remaining natural resources on Earth and produce so much pollution and overpopulation that the whole world's society will collapse. Resources will run out. Food and industrial production will tumble. The death rate will climb out of sight. Mass starvation, war, pestilence.

All this was shown on clear, inexorable-looking graphs, straight from the computer's printout.

The graphs showed that the curves representing population, industrial production, farm output, and natural resources all reach peaks early in the Twenty-First Century, then collapse.

Superdisaster.

And it's very real, if you grant a few critical assumptions.

The MIT study (which was sponsored by an international organization called The Club of Rome) evoked immediate howls of protest from some people, and smiles of delight from others. Some said the book was a mathematically-accurate forecast, and we must work hard to avert the doom that it predicts. Others said that it was a grab-bag of poor assumptions and muddled thinking. As I'm writing this, more than a year after the publication of *The Limits to Growth* and in the midst of a growing energy crisis, the argument is still raging on university campuses and in the halls of governments all around the world. And the clock ticks on.

Most people were caught by surprise when the book came out. Many refused to believe that a disaster is possible. It's too shocking for them to accept. But science fiction people were neither surprised nor outraged. The study was actually old news to them. They had been making their own "models" of tomorrow and testing them all their lives.

(Incidentally, several science fiction writers, including Arthur C. Clarke, immediately pointed out that the MIT scientists automatically assumed that the Earth is a closed ecological system. They didn't consider that humankind now has the ability to draw natural resources from other bodies in the solar system. This is perhaps the biggest flaw in the study.)

What the scientists did with their computer is very much like the thing that science fiction writers and readers have been doing for decades. But instead of using a computer to "model" future world societies, science fiction writers have used their human imaginations. This human resource gives them some enormous advantages.

One of the advantages is flexibility.

Science fiction writers are not in the business of predicting THE future. They do something much more important. They try to show all the many possible futures that lie open to us. If the history of the human race can be pictured as an enormous migration through time, with thousands of millions of people wandering through the centuries, then the writers of science fiction are the scouts, the explorers, the adventurers who go out ahead and look over the landscape, then send back stories that warn of the harsh desert up ahead, or tales that dazzle us with reports of the beautiful mountains and forests that lie just over the horizon.

For there is not simply a future, a time to come that's preordained and inexorable. Our future is built, bit by bit, minute by minute, by the actions of human beings. One vital role that science fiction plays is to show us what kinds of future might result from certain kinds of human actions.

Have you ever stood on a flat sandy beach, at the edge of the water, and watched the little wavelets play at your feet? After the breakers have dumped their energy and the water has rushed as far up the beach as it can go, there's a crisscross pattern of wavelets that mottle the beach. If the sun's at the proper angle, you can clearly see what physicists call *interference patterns*. The wavelets interact with one another, sometimes adding together to form a stronger wave, sometimes cancelling each other to form a blank spot in the pattern.

The myriads of ideas that parade across the pages of science fiction magazines and books form such a pattern for SF readers and writers. Some ideas get reinforced, added to, strengthened by repetition and enlargement. Other ideas fall out of favor, because they're found to be lacking in one way or another by SF readers.

Thus, for more than a generation now, science fiction people have been worrying about the problems of pollution, nuclear warfare, overpopulation, genetic manipulation, runaway technology, thought control, and other threats that are just now bursting on the awareness of the general public as shocking surprises.

Other potential problems have been examined and dropped. Today there are few stories about invisible men seized with dreams of power. Or plagues of "space germs" infecting the Earth. When Michael Crichton's *Andromeda Strain* became a vastly popular book and movie, most science fiction people groaned, "But it's an old idea!" Meaning that it's no longer an *interesting* idea; the problem does not and probably will not exist. But this old idea of "the plague from space" was shatteringly new and exciting to the general public.

To communicate the ideas, the fears and hopes, the shape and feel of all the infinitely possible futures, science fiction writers lean heavily on the second of their major advantages: the art of fiction, or storytelling.

Although a scientist's job is just about finished when he's reduced his data to tabular or graphic form, the work of a science fiction writer is just then beginning. His task is to convey the human story. The scientific basis for the possible future in his story is merely the background. Perhaps "merely" is too limiting a word. Many science fiction stories consist of precious little except the background, the basic idea, the gimmick. But the best of science fiction, the stories that make a lasting impact on generations of readers, are stories about *people*.

As we saw in Chapter Four, the "people" may be nonhuman. They may be robots or aliens with tentacle and six eyes. But they will be people in the sense that human readers can feel sympathy for them, share their joys, sorrows, dangers, and triumphs.

The basic art of storytelling hasn't really changed much since prehistoric times, because our nervous systems haven't changed, and that's what determines the kinds of information we can receive and deal with, in our minds.

From the earliest Biblical tales, through Homer to Shakespeare, and right down to today's commercial fiction industry, the formula for telling a powerful story has remained the same: Create a strong character, a person of great strengths, capable of deep emotions and decisive action. Give him a weakness. Set him in conflict with another powerful character—or in conflict with nature. Let this exterior conflict be the mirror of the character's own internal struggle, the clash of his desires, his own strength pitted against his own weakness. And there you have a story.

Whether it's Abraham offering his only son to God, or Paris bringing ruin to Troy over Helen, or Hamlet and Claudius playing their deadly game, or Faust seeking the world's knowledge and power, D.D. Harriman, Montag the Fireman, Michael Valentine Smith, Maud'Dib—the stories that stand out in the minds of the readers are those that are made incandescent by the burning brilliance of their characters, people who are unforgettable.

To show other worlds, to describe possible future societies, or to predict the problems lurking ahead is not enough. A reader gets quickly bored with dry unemotional tracts. The writer of science fiction must show how these worlds and these futures affect human beings.

And something much more important: The science fiction writer must show how human beings can and do create these future worlds.

For our future is largely in our own hands. It doesn't come rolling blindly out of the heavens; it is the joint product of the actions of billions of human beings. This is a point that's easily forgotten in the rush of headlines and the hectic badgering of everyday life. But it's a point that good science fiction makes constantly: The future belongs to us, whatever it is. We make it, our actions shape tomorrow.

We have the brains and guts to build paradise, or at least to try. Tragedy is when we try and fail. The greatest crime of all is when we fail even to try.

Thus science fiction stands as a bridge between science and art, between the engineers of technology and the poets of humanity. Never has such a bridge been needed more desperately.

In that same year, 1972, the famed poet and historian Robert Graves wrote in the British journal, *New Scientist:* "Technology is now warring openly against the crafts, and science covertly against poetry."

Graves was expressing a fear that many people share: Technology has already allowed machines to replace human muscle power. Now it seems that machines such as electronic computers might replace human brain power, as well. But he went even further, pointing a shaking finger at science as the wellspring of technology, and criticizing science for allowing technology to get so powerful.

He went on to say that science isn't as "human" an activity as poetry, because it is usually the product of intuitive thinking, which—Graves said —"scientists would dismiss . . . as 'illogical.' "

Graves apparently sees scientists as a sober, plodding phalanx of soulless thinking machines, never making a step that hadn't been carefully thought out in advance. He's forgotten about Archimedes.

As an historian, Graves should know what a powerful role intuition has played in science. As a poet, he ought to realize that scientists are human beings. They are just as human, as intuitive, as emotional as anyone else. But most people don't realize this. They don't know scientists, any more than they know much about science.

C. P. Snow pointed out in the 1950's that there is a gap between the Two Cultures—science and art. Graves' remarks show that the gap is widening into a painful chasm. Graves is a scholar and should know better. He's justly renowned for his work in ancient mythology, where he's combined his talents in poetry and historical research in a truly original and beautiful way.

But he doesn't seem to understand that scientists do exactly the same thing.

We've seen that since the Ice Age days of tribal shamans, most people have held highly ambivalent attitudes toward the medicine man-astrologer-wizard-scientist. Before the general public can understand and appreciate what science can and cannot do, the people must get to see and understand the scientists themselves. Get to know their work, their aims, their dreams, and their fears.

A possible way of humanizing science and scientists comes from the field in which Graves made his major effort: mythology.

Joseph Campbell, Professor of Literature at Sarah Lawrence College, has spent a good deal of his life studying humankind's mythologies. He's pointed out that modern man has no modern mythology to turn to. The old myths are dead, and no really new mythology has arisen to take their place. Unfortunately, Professor Campbell is not a science fiction reader.

Human beings need mythology, Campbell insists. A well-structured mythology gives a sort of emotional meaning and stability to a person's life. Myths are a sort of rulebook, on an emotional level, that shows a person what's expected of him in his attitudes toward life, death, and the whole vast and sometimes scary universe.

An example: Almost every primitive society has a Prometheus myth. In our western culture, the Greek version is the one most quoted. Prometheus was a demigod who saw that man was a weak, starving, freezing creature, barely able to survive among the animals of the woods and fields. Taking pity on man, Prometheus stole fire from the heavens and gave it to man, at the cost of a horrible punishment to himself. But man, with fire, became master of the Earth.

A typical myth, fantastic in detail yet absolutely correct in spirit. One of man's early ancestors tamed fire about a half-million years ago, as we saw in

Chapter Two. Most likely these primitive *Homo erectus* creatures saw lightning flash a tree or shrub into flame: hence the legend of the gift from the heavens. Before fire, our ancestors were merely another marginal anthropoid, most of whom died away eventually. With fire, we've become the dominant species on this planet.

The Prometheus myth "explains" this titanic event in terms that primitive people can understand and accept. The myth gives emotional underpinning to the bald facts, and ties reality into a system of thinking that explains both the known and incomprehensible parts of human experience.

Today, hardly anyone believes such myths. Much of our modern emotional energy is spent on other things, and we have not developed a new mythology that can explain the modern world on a gut level to people who are frightened and bewildered by the complexities and dangers of our society.

Part of the reason for science fiction's mushrooming popularity is that SF fills the role of a modern mythology.

Joseph Campbell's work has shown that there are at least four major functions of any mythology.

First, a mythology must induce a feeling of awe and majesty in people. This is what science fiction people call "a sense of wonder," and it is the hallmark of a well-received SF story.

Second, a mythology must set up and uphold a system of the universe, a pattern of self-consistent explanation for both the known and incomprehensible parts of man's existence. In science fiction, this system is science itself: a continuously-expanding body of knowledge about the universe.

Third, a mythology usually supports the social establishment. For example, what we today call Greek mythology apparently originated with the Achaean conquerors of the earlier Mycenaean civilization that dwelled in the lands and islands around the Aegean Sea.

Zeus was the Achaean sky god who conquered the matriarchal goddesses of the Mycenaean agricultural cities. Most of the romantic legends about Zeus' amorous entanglements with local goddesses are explanations of the barbaric, patriarchal Achaeans' overwhelming the Mycenaean matriarchies.

Fourth, a mythology serves as an emotional crutch to help the individual member of the society to get through the inevitable crises of life, such as the transition from childhood into adulthood, and the inescapable prospect of death.

Science fiction, when it's at its very best, can serve these functions of a modern mythology.

Certainly science fiction tries to induce a sense of wonder about the physical universe and man's own interior private universe of the mind. Science fiction depends heavily on known scientific understanding as the basic underpinning of a universal order.

Science fiction doesn't tend to support any particular political establishment, but on a deeper level it almost invariably backs the basic tenets of individuality that form the backbone of western civilization; that is, the concept that the individual person is worth more than the Organization, whatever it may be. In most SF stories, nothing is more important than individual freedom.

Whether or not science fiction helps people through emotional crises is more difficult to tell. But it's interesting to see that science fiction has a huge readership among the young, the adolescents who are trying to figure out their own individual places in the universe. And how many science fiction stories about superheroes and time travel and immortality are actually an attempt to blunt the brutal fact that death awaits each one of us?

On this emotional level, science fiction can and does serve the functions of mythology. On a more cerebral, conscious level, science fiction helps to explain what science and scientists are all about to the non-scientists. It's no accident that several hundred universities are now offering science fiction courses, and discovering that these classes are a meeting ground for the scientist-engineers and the liberal arts humanists. Science *and* fiction. Reason *and* emotion.

The essence of the scientific attitude is that the human mind can succeed in understanding the universe. By taking thought, humans can move mountains—and have. In this sense, science is utterly humanistic. It is the glorification of human intellect over the puzzling, chaotic, and often frightening darkness of ignorance.

Much of science fiction celebrates this spirit. Although there are plenty of SF stories that warn of the dangers of science and technology—the Frankenstein, dystopia (anti-utopia) stories—there are many, many more that look to science and technology for the leverage by which human beings can move the world. Even in the darkest, gloomiest, most downbeat dystopia stories there is usually some aura of striving, some attempt to achieve greatness. Very few science fiction stories picture humanity as a passive species, allowing the tidal forces of nature to overwhelm us. The heroes in SF stories struggle bravely against the darkness, whether it's geological doom for the whole planet or the evil of grasping politicians. They may not always win, these SF heroes, but they always *try*.

Perhaps this is the dual role of science fiction: to serve as a new mythology, and to act as an interpreter of science and scientists to the non-scientific public. To accomplish this, science fiction stories must boldly go where the readers have never set foot before.

All too often, science fiction writers become painfully aware of how little their fellow-humans understand the universe in general, and SF in particular. Since July 20, 1969, just about every SF writer in the world must have been asked at least once:

"Now that we've reached the Moon, what's left for you fellows to write about?"

Isaac Asimov, never at a loss for a rejoinder, coined the classic answer for that inane question. Thinking of Mars, of the hundred billion stars of our Milky Way galaxy and the hundred billion galaxies beyond, of the mysteries still locked inside the atom's elementary particles, of the endless labyrinths of the human mind, Asimov replied:

"What's left to write about? Only everything!"

Permissions granted for
the illustrations in this book
are as follows:

Page 49•Copyright © 1940
in U.S.A. and Great Britain by
Street & Smith Publication's, Inc.
Copyright © 1968 by
The Condé Nast Publications Inc.
for July 1940 cover.

Page 50•Copyright 1942 by Popular
Publications Inc. Used by permission.

Page 51•Walter Hortens

Page 52•Richard M. Sternbach

Earth or any portions thereof
Jacket, cover, pages 1, 3, 4–5, 10, 11,
34, 35, 63, 84, 85, 104, 105, 122, 124–125
National Aeronautics and Space Administration

Rear endpaper No. 1•Frank Kelly Freas

Rear endpaper No. 2•Frank Kelly Freas

City skyline on jacket and cover•Rhode Island School of Design

Index

ABOUT THE AUTHOR

Ben Bova is as well-known for his science-fact books as for science fiction, and at times the two fields almost seem to merge. Currently editor of the most widely read and influential science fiction magazine in the world, *Analog*, Mr. Bova is also a consultant with Avco Everett Research Laboratory. His work at Avco takes him to the frontiers of current scientific investigation and he utilizes his experience and knowledge as a lecturer on a wide range of topics.

SCIENCE FICTION

analog

SCIENCE FACT

DECEMBER 1969 **60c** (6/-)

SRUTTEN

IN OUR HANDS, THE STARS

Harry Harrison